Birthday present from Jan.

WHO BY FIRE

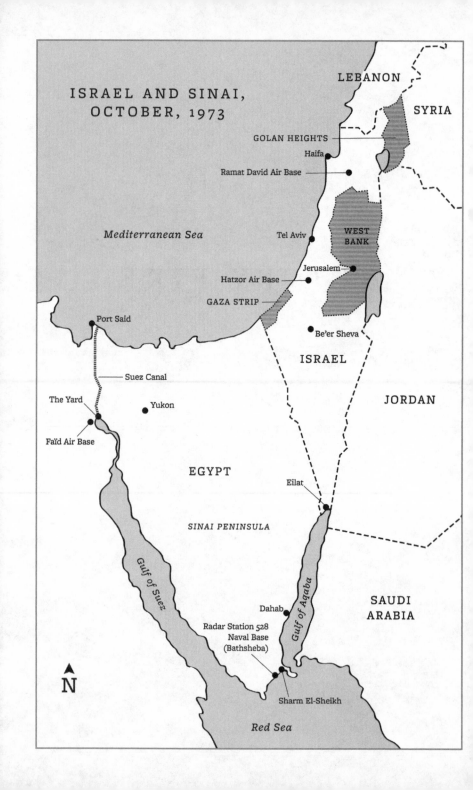

WHO BY FIRE

WAR, ATONEMENT, AND THE
RESURRECTION OF LEONARD COHEN

MATTI FRIEDMAN

SIGNAL
McCLELLAND
& STEWART

Hardcover edition published 2022

Signal and colophon are registered trademarks of Penguin Random House
Canada Limited.

Published simultaneously in the United States of America by Spiegel & Grau LLC.

Library and Archives Canada Cataloguing in Publication data is available
upon request.

ISBN: 978-0-7710-9626-6
ebook ISBN: 978-0-7710-9627-3

Owing to limitations of space, photography acknowledgements appear on
pages 225–226.

Jacket and book design by Andrew Roberts
Jacket art: Isaac Shokal
Typeset by M&S, Toronto

Printed in Canada

Published by Signal,
an imprint of McClelland & Stewart,
a division of Penguin Random House Canada Limited,
a Penguin Random House Company

www.penguinrandomhouse.ca

1   2   3   4   5   26   25   24   23   22

Welcome to these lines
There is a war on
But I'll try to make you comfortable

L. COHEN

CONTENTS

WHO BY FIRE

INTRODUCTION

Some of the men on the sand look up at the visitor with his guitar. Others look down at their dirty knees and boots. Cigarettes glow in the dark. The heat has broken and the desert is still for now. They've been fighting for fourteen days and no one knows how many days are left, or how many of them will be left when it's over. There aren't any generals or heroes here. It's just a small unit getting smaller. In the wastelands around them, thousands of Egyptians and Israelis are dead.

The visitor, dressed in khaki, is Leonard Cohen. This makes little sense to anyone at the outer extremity of the Sinai front in the Yom Kippur War of October 1973. Not long ago he was playing for a half million people at the Isle of Wight Festival, which was bigger than Woodstock. Here it's a few dozen. None of the soldiers know how Leonard Cohen came to be here with them, or why.

Cohen is thirty-nine. He's been brought low and thinks he's finished. News of his retirement has appeared in the music press. "I just feel like I want to shut up. Just shut up," he told an interviewer. He might have come to this country and this war looking for some desperate way out of his dead end, a way to transcend everything and sing again. If that's what he was looking for, he seems to have found it, as we'll see. Five decades later, on Spotify and in synagogue, you can still hear the echo of this trip. Anyone reading these lines remembers the elderly gentleman grinning out from under a fedora at packed concert halls around the world, and knows that in 1973 his greatest acts are yet to come. But right now this isn't clear to him or to anyone else.

Cohen addresses the soldiers in solemn English. A reporter who is there describes the scene in a dispatch for a Hebrew music magazine. In the yellowing newsprint you can tell the reporter is a cynic. He mocks the star as "the great pacifist" come from abroad, a glorified tourist. A reader has the impression that the reporter doesn't want to be moved but is.

When the soldiers join Cohen for the chorus of "So Long, Marianne," their voices are the only sound in the desert. He introduces the next number. "This song is one that should be heard at home, in a warm room with a drink and a woman you love," he says. "I hope you all find yourselves in that situation soon." He plays "Suzanne." The men are quiet. They hear about a place that doesn't have blackened tanks and figures lying still in charred coveralls. It's a city by a river, a perfect body, tea and oranges all the way from China. "They're listening to his music," writes the reporter, "but who knows where their thoughts are wandering."

Sometimes an artist and an event interact to generate a spark far bigger than both: art that isn't a mere memorial to whatever inspired it, but an assertion of human creativity in the face of all inhuman events. It isn't necessary to know the convoluted course of Spain's civil war to grasp Picasso's *Guernica*. A listener can wonder at Beethoven's Fifth Symphony, composed amid the Napoleonic Wars, without recognizing the bars of a French revolutionary song hidden in one of the movements. It's possible to appreciate the beauty of a shard of glass without knowing how the window looked before it was smashed, or what the moment of shattering was like. But it seems to me that if we can know, our understanding is enriched—not just our understanding of a momentous occurrence or of the personality of an artist, but of the nature of inspiration, and of art's supernatural ability to fly through years and places and lodge in distant minds, helping us rise beyond ourselves.

The moment, in this case, was a concert tour, maybe one of the greatest, certainly one of the strangest. The tour might have produced a celebrated rock documentary or live album— but no one thought to film it and hardly any recordings survive. It happened in the midst of an Israeli war but isn't documented in the country's military records. The account you just read is the only description of any of the concerts to appear in print at the time, and even that magazine, a local version of *Rolling Stone*, has been defunct for years. The tour has lived on as underground history—in word of mouth, in photographs snapped by soldiers, in notebooks filed in an office on Wilshire Boulevard in Los Angeles, in a box of papers in Hamilton, Ontario, and recorded between the lines of a few great songs. Reconstructing what happened has meant piecing together these scraps over many years.

While no detailed account has appeared before, and while this cultural moment is known even to Cohen's fans as a footnote, if at all, its importance keeps growing in a curious way. Here in Israel, for example, before the anniversary of the war every fall, more and more articles appear in the press, as if the story must be told and retold each year. Some of the descriptions are repetitive or inaccurate. But all are genuine expressions of the fact that the memory of that terrible month, October 1973, has somehow become linked to the strange appearance of Leonard Cohen.

If Cohen's tour is now part of the Yom Kippur War, the war itself is inseparable from a date in the Jewish calendar. The fighting began with a surprise attack by Syria and Egypt at two p.m. on the Day of Atonement, when Jewish tradition demands introspection and tells us that our fates are decided for the coming year—who will die, and how. The symbolism here is so clumsy that it seems to beg an apology.

The war's timing has lent a kind of awful grandeur to the grim proceedings. In fact the war is sometimes called the War of Atonement, as if it were itself a penance for the pride and blindness that preceded it, for the failures of leadership that left Israeli soldiers exposed on October 6, 1973, when the Syrian army attacked through the basalt outcroppings of the Golan Heights and the Egyptians across the sand embankments of the Suez Canal. Israel's judgment had been clouded by victory in the Six-Day War, six years earlier, and the country had allowed itself to sink into arrogance and complacency. The borders were defended by a handful of ill-fated infantrymen and tank crews.

For a few desperate days on the Golan plateau there were nearly no Israeli troops left between the Syrians and Israel's heartland beneath the heights, in Galilee. On the southern front, the one of interest to us here, the Egyptians captured the Israeli outposts along the Suez Canal, drove into Sinai, and shredded the defenders' frantic counterattacks. Israel's air force, which was supposed to win the war, was instead crippled by new Soviet missiles, and within days the defence minister, the one-eyed war hero Moshe Dayan, was heard despairing that the "Third Temple is in danger," meaning Israel itself. Only with extraordinary exertion, and at the cost of more than 2,600 fatalities, did the soldiers in the field turn the war around and, by the end of the month, deliver a victory that still felt like a defeat.

When the battles ended, the prestige of Israel's generals and political leaders, the icons of the founding genera-tion, was shattered. The country became less confident, less united, and more introspective; after the war this was, in many ways, a different country. The mistakes would be picked apart in hundreds of anguished memoirs and critical histories whose publication began at the end of the war and continues to this day. When I served in an Israeli infantry unit twenty-five years later, our training involved imaginary battles against columns of enemy tanks invading through the desert, a scenario which had little to do with the actual war-fare of the late 1990s—it was recognizably Yom Kippur, the war the army was still fighting in its mind.

For people in Israel, the ancient fast day and the dark anni-versary of the war are so intertwined that they can no longer be detached. And so Leonard Cohen—who many considered a poet of cigarettes and sex and quiet human desperation, who'd dismissed the Jewish community that raised him as a vessel of empty ritual, who despised violence and thought little of states—made himself not only part of this Israeli war but of the most solemn day of the Jewish calendar. How this all came to pass has never been explained: the meeting of young soldiers at a moment of extreme peril with one of the great voices of the age. That's the subject of this book.

One of the oddest aspects of this episode is that Cohen almost never mentioned it afterward. This fact seemed stranger and stranger to me the more I discovered about how deep he went into the war, and how significant the experience was for the people who saw him. There are a few comments to the music magazine *ZigZag* in London a few months later, when he was asked explicitly, but not much more. The same seems to have been true in private: people who were close to Cohen don't remember ever hearing the details. Cohen's concern wasn't history but the soul. He might have felt that a link to real events would reduce his work to mere journalism. "For me, poetry is the evidence of a life, and not the life itself. It's the ashes of something that's burning well," Cohen once said. "Sometimes you confuse yourself and try to create ashes instead of fire." In this case, the war was just the fire. It wasn't his business to explain how many logs went in and how hot it burned, or how close he was standing. Some beautiful ashes came of it, and that's enough.

It turns out, however, that Cohen did leave an account of those weeks. It is, as you might expect, remarkable, but it was never published. It's a manuscript of forty-five type-written pages in a box at the McMaster University library in Hamilton, outside Toronto, in the archive of McClelland & Stewart, the venerable Canadian house that was his publisher. The pages aren't a finished product. They were the larval stage of a project he called "My Life in Art," which evolved into a book of poetry called *Death of a Lady's Man*, published five years after the war. A few fragments of the original manuscript appeared there as individual poems, and the rest was forgotten.

Parts of this document seem to be the early draft of a work of fiction, one written in the heightened emotional style of the early novels, like *The Favourite Game*, which Cohen wrote before turning to music. The manuscript is written in the first person. Though the material is so raw that the true events and characters are barely concealed, or entirely unconcealed, we're not necessarily meant to mistake this "I" for the literal Leonard Cohen. Other sections of the manuscript consist of clear summaries of events in point form, sketches of episodes that Cohen might have planned to flesh out later, but never did. These seem to be accurate descriptions, close to journal entries.

The work of triangulating the facts in this manuscript involved the second trove of Cohen material that I used for this book—the pocket notebooks he kept around the time of the war, to which I was granted access by the Cohen estate in Los Angeles. Compared to the hundreds of notebooks Cohen kept throughout his life, the ones from the war are meagre, implying that the poet was diverted by these events, perhaps disturbed by them, and that his introspective flow was unusually disrupted. The notebooks suggest that even if the narrator of the literary manuscript is a fictionalized version of Cohen, the events are mostly factual. For example, one might suspect that the characters who serve obvious literary functions are inventions. But in the notebooks you can find their phone numbers and addresses.

That makes it possible, with all necessary caution, to treat the literary manuscript as Cohen's immediate attempt to put into words what he'd just seen. The document gives us a version of Cohen's voice that is very different from the polished and evasive one he used in interviews. With this resource at my disposal, and with the estate's rare permission to publish it for the first time, I'm lucky enough to be able, at several points in this book, to simply turn over the microphone and let Cohen tell the story himself.

A great rock tour tends to follow a familiar story line: adulation, decadence, chaos, collapse, musical redemption. This one wasn't like that, or like any other tour. The connection between the musician and the landscape, for example, was unique: Cohen, an artist formed by the language of the Hebrew Bible as a child growing up in a Montreal synagogue, the grandson of a learned rabbi, was playing the wilderness around Mount Sinai. The names in the war could have been taken from his poems, like "Israel" and "Egypt," or "Babylon," which here is an intelligence base under a mountain. In this story there's a soldier named Isaac, and a lieutenant named for the warrior-king David. There's even a Bathsheba, the woman David saw bathing on her roof, whose "beauty in the moonlight overthrew" him, and who the king loved so deeply that he sent her husband to die in a war. (Here "Bathsheba" is not a woman but a naval landing craft slated for a suicide raid.) A parallel in rock music might be Springsteen playing the tracks from *Greetings from Asbury Park, N.J.* in Asbury Park, N.J., or the Beatles doing a free concert at Strawberry Fields.

Cohen wasn't from here. But he called Israel his "myth home," and being here seemed to trigger a fevered consideration of who he was and what he owed to others—the woman waiting for him with his child on a Greek island, his family, the Jews. It's not quite clear what he meant by "myth home," or if even he understood what he meant. But it's clear this wasn't just another gig.

More than anything, what made this tour exceptional was the audience. A singer whose themes were human imperfection and transience, and the brief pleasures that can sweeten your night, found himself in front of people for whom those weren't abstractions floated into the air of a dorm room. They knew death was waiting for them when the concert ended. He played for them knowing his music might be the last thing they heard. So while a typical report on a concert tour would focus on the artist, with the audience appearing as a sea of blurry faces or a muted roar of applause, that can't be the case here. I've spent several years looking for people who encountered Cohen during those weeks and trying to understand what happened to them before and after the show. More information about the characters, the chronology, and my sources can be found in the notes at the end of the book.

Each concert was a pure artistic transmission. No money changed hands. No one sold tickets or bought records. Many of the soldiers didn't know English, and Cohen couldn't speak Hebrew, but T.S. Eliot is right that poetry, when it's good, "can communicate before it is understood." In photographs the singer seems transported and the audience intent. This isn't Woodstock. It isn't a night out. Everyone's sober. The stakes are high. Something important is happening.

1

RADAR STATION 528,
SHARM EL-SHEIKH

The nocturnal activity of the air force at the southern tip
of the Sinai Peninsula, end of summer 1973: A flash of
white thigh in dark water. Hair plastered down a smooth back.
Ripples glimmering around rocks. Bras and fatigues crumpled
on the sand.

Desert mountains surged from the interior to hover like
frozen breakers over the shore, the Red Sea stretched south
toward Yemen, and two armies faced each other along the
Suez Canal, but you couldn't see any of it in the dark. The
scene was just a half dozen soldiers in a cove. Because in this
memory they're naked, they don't even look like soldiers, just
teenagers. Their doomed radar station is out of sight.

In the memories of the people who served there, Sharm
el-Sheikh was sprinkled with stardust. They all recall the time
before the war with the same faraway look and half smile.

Ruti, Pnina, and Orly are all grandmothers now, but in the photographs they're nineteen and smiling. Everything's about to happen.

The photos show beaches and blistering sunlight in seventies Kodachrome, and kids in civilian bell-bottoms. Sometimes they're in khaki pants or regulation miniskirts in a nod to the military that sent them here, but the military seemed to be beside the point. There was one hut between the airstrip and the water where the guys were known for the grouper they caught in the gulf and would grill for you if you showed up, especially if you were a girl; their official designation was "Reception," but no one knew what they were receiving. In the photos they're all playing guitars or mugging in aviator shades, or standing at one spot by the airfield where the desert wind in the evening was better than any blow dryer. It seems like a combination of the original *Charlie's Angels* and *M*A*S*H*, shot in the landscape of the Book of Exodus.

The mood wasn't just the confidence left over from the victory six years earlier, when Sharm el-Sheikh and the rest of Sinai came under Israeli control, but also the youth, optimism, and togetherness of the sixties. In America it was already the autumn of Watergate. It had been four years since the bloodshed at the Stones' Altamont Speedway show symbolically ended the Age of Aquarius. The Summer of Love was a memory. But in those days everything reached Israel late, and here the sixties lasted into 1973, until October 6.

Ruti ran the telephone switchboard at the airfield. In her photos she's surrounded by friends and admirers, posing in her uniform and Star of David necklace, stretched on a rock in a bikini. In some of her pictures there's a soldier named Doron. He was moody and had an unmilitary mop of black hair that threw shade over his eyes. He wrote dark teenage poetry about a girl he longed for but whose name he didn't specify. Doron grew up poor in Haifa after his parents escaped the country called "the Holocaust." (Where are your parents from? From the Holocaust.) These kids didn't have much to do with that. They were the first generation of native "Israelis"— not tortured, not a minority, not religious, not exactly Jews, but creatures sprung from sunlight and salt water.

Doron was handsome and Ruti wanted to know him better, but at first he spoke sharply to her and kept his distance. He wouldn't party like the others. Instead he'd sit on a ladder near the runway to watch the propeller planes that ferried soldiers from Israel across the desert to this distant outpost, their passengers emerging from air-conditioning into the heat pulsing from the asphalt. Once, when he thought Ruti was too slow to patch him through her switchboard, he lost his temper and shouted at her. But a few months in paradise softened him, and they became friends. In the following photograph she's holding the guitar and he's next to her, shirtless.

Pnina and Orly monitored screens at the radar station that sat above the airfield, on a mountain that rose like a long blade from the desert floor. The radars looked into Egyptian airspace, and on the screens enemy planes appeared as yellow dots. Pnina was the senior girl at the station, and Orly was a bit younger, with the soul of an artist. (The radar monitors were men and women ranging from their late teens to early

twenties, but even decades later they refer to themselves at the time as "girls" and "boys," and because this isn't far from the truth I'll preserve their language here.) The Egyptians had been defeated so thoroughly six years earlier, the humiliation of their air force so complete, that the yellow dots kept a safe distance from Israeli airspace. None of the radar monitors had ever seen a real enemy plane.

Under the screens were Perspex tables where they could write out coordinates with erasable markers. Orly was sometimes so bored that she used the Perspex to copy lines of Hebrew poetry from memory. She especially liked the work of Rachel, a poet of the pioneer generation of the 1920s who'd lived on the shore of Lake Kinneret, her awareness sharpened by terminal tuberculosis. "I'll line my basket with

Kinneret memories," she wrote in her poem "Gift": "The pink of the morning sky among the garden trees / The afternoon gold in a peaceful clearing / The evening jasmine on the Golan hills." Rachel was sad but never cynical. She didn't have a husband or children, and she was young and dying, but she had the beauty of the land and of the act of living in it. Orly can still recite these lines by heart decades later. Between shifts, the monitors would smoke in the sandbag emplacements overlooking the Red Sea. They had a phonograph and a few records—some Hebrew albums, one in Spanish, and one Leonard Cohen.

———

One of the laws given by God to Moses at Mount Sinai, according to Jewish tradition, mandates a day of atonement and fasting every year on the tenth day of the seventh month, a "Sabbath of Sabbaths." The mountain commonly identified as the site of this revelation is about fifty miles from the cove where the soldiers went skinny-dipping. In 1973, the eve of Yom Kippur fell on October 5.

In a prefab hut at the airfield was a small synagogue with some tattered prayer books and army-issue skullcaps. Ruti went to services that evening. Like many Jews who think little of religious observance most of the year, she took this day seriously. Yom Kippur begins at sundown and ends the following night, when the gate of heaven closes with a final prayer called "the Locking." You can't eat or drink anything in between. But when Ruti finished the first evening prayer and returned to the room she shared with a few other girls, still in a contemplative mood, she wrote in her diary that boys from the airfield's maintenance crew were resolutely ignoring their religion: "The bastards were having a nice big meal."

The next day's observance keeps you in synagogue almost from morning to night. The service, many hundreds of Hebrew pages, is like a slow drive through rolling liturgical countryside. It meanders for miles, crawling through land so featureless it can put you to sleep, hooking back on itself so that you wonder if you didn't pass that same red barn an hour ago. But there are several peaks that offer a flash of understanding and a view of something great and old. Three of these moments have become permanently linked in my own mind to Leonard Cohen, and to this story, and so are worth mentioning here.

One moment is a prayer called Unetaneh Tokef, which is about one thousand years old, though no one knows for sure. The prayer describes God's judgment and the insignificance of human beings who are "like a broken shard, like dry grass, a withered flower, like a passing shadow and a vanishing cloud, like a breeze that blows away and dust that scatters, like a dream that flits away." The name of the prayer, translated as "Let us relate the power," comes from its opening phrase, "Let us relate the power of this day's holiness." On Yom Kippur, the prayer tells us, it is sealed:

> *How many will pass on and how many be created,*
> *Who will live and who will die,*
> *Who will reach the end of their days and who will not,*
> *Who by water and who by fire,*

Who by sword and who by wild beast,
Who by famine and who by thirst . . .

The lines aren't sophisticated, they're crude, but in the same way that life is crude. The symbolism is violent and memorable.

Another moment, a remnant of the service in the Jerusalem Temple that was destroyed by Rome in the year 70 CE, comes when men who are descended from the priestly class, the *Cohanim*, get up to bless the congregation. They stand in a line at the front of the synagogue, part their fingers in the middle in a mystic sign, and cloak themselves in prayer shawls so you can't see their faces, maybe so you don't know that the "priests" are just Mr. Cohen your gym teacher, or your friend's dad. For a moment, the tradition transforms them into something noble. They recite a blessing that consists of fifteen Hebrew words: "May God bless you and guard you. May God shine His face upon you and be gracious to you. May God lift up His face to you and grant you peace." It's a very old blessing. The same text was dug up near my neighbourhood in Jerusalem on a silver amulet that someone engraved 2,600 years ago.

The third and final moment comes in the afternoon, when the energies of the congregation are flagging and everyone's lips are dry. This is the reading of the Book of Jonah, the greatest story ever told in forty-eight sentences. In this story, God tries to speak to a man named Jonah, who runs away. Jonah is the only prophet in the Bible who does that. It's the opposite of the way Abraham, in the Book of Genesis, responds to a similar call. Abraham says, "Here I am." In Hebrew that's just one word: *hineini*. God tells Abraham to build an altar to sacrifice his son, Isaac, and Abraham does. *Hineini*. Other prophets plead unsuitability at first, like Moses, who tells God that he stutters, and Jeremiah, who protests that he's too young. But Jonah is the only one who tries to escape.

Instead of going east to warn the sinful metropolis of Nineveh to repent, as God wants, Jonah catches a boat sailing from Jaffa west to Tarshish, whose precise location isn't known but doesn't really matter—it's just somewhere far away in the Mediterranean, in the direction opposite of the one intended for him. The rest of the story is about Jonah learning that escape is impossible. A storm nearly sinks his ship and he's thrown overboard, then swallowed by a fish and spit out on shore, until we finally find him alone in the unforgiving sun of the desert outside Nineveh. A miraculous plant that sprang up instantly and gave him shade has withered and died with equal speed, and now there's no shade, no port, no boat. It's just Jonah and the overwhelming presence of God, who decides who'll live and die, who by water and who by thirst. That's where the story leaves Jonah, and us, as the Day of Atonement nears its end. The tradition shuts off our usual escape routes—food, work, sex, screens—and tries to move us from Jonah's mindset at the beginning of the story to his understanding at the end. It's an understanding that's hard for most of us to grasp, but not for people who are very old, or very ill, or in a war.

On the morning of Yom Kippur, Ruti didn't make it to the airfield's synagogue. According to her diary entry for

October 6, she slept late in the bed of the dark, broad-chested technician who was her boyfriend at the time. So she didn't hear Unetaneh Tokef, or the priestly blessing.

At 1:51 p.m. one of the radios crackled at Babylon; under a hill elsewhere in Sinai; in a bunker full of speakers, unwashed tea glasses, and tense Israelis in green fatigues. An intelligence lieutenant named David heard an Egyptian pilot speaking in clipped Arabic, reporting an attack run. David shouted, "They're coming." Someone pressed an emergency button. All the Egyptian frequencies at Babylon came alive. *Allahu akbar*, they were shouting: God is great.

Artillery shells carpeted the Israeli side of the Suez Canal and thousands of Egyptian soldiers swarmed across the waterway. At the same moment, far away in the north of Israel, Syrian soldiers and tanks surged through minefields into the Golan Heights. An Egyptian bomber over the Mediterranean fired a guided missile at Tel Aviv.

Ruti heard the siren go off at the airfield, a sound that all Israelis know: a moan that starts low, clenches your stomach, then climbs in tone for two or three seconds, giving you time to realize that something bad is happening, and to wonder what it's going to mean for you. The same siren was sounding across Israel and everyone who was here that day remembers it, the way the worshippers fell silent in the synagogues and strangers looked at each other on the street.

Two Phantoms stood on the runway near Ruti's hut, new American jets with blue Stars of David painted on their wings. The air crews at Sharm el-Sheikh were theoretically on alert, but like everyone else in the air force, they associated the base with girls, guitars, and barbecues. It was supposed to be a place to unwind. The pilots and navigators had spent the previous night using what they called "the most important weapon in the sector," the base's 16-millimetre movie projector. In one of those details that would stretch the author's credibility in a work of fiction, they watched *Tora! Tora! Tora!*, a Hollywood epic about the surprise attack at Pearl Harbor.

Ruti was standing outside when the engines screamed toward her overhead. The two Phantoms took off and disappeared into the sky. New planes appeared, and she remembered Doron the black-haired poet and a few other boys shouting that these ones weren't ours, which didn't make sense to her even when an Egyptian bomb cratered the asphalt a hundred yards away. She kicked off her sandals and ran barefoot for shelter. A story from the victory of 1967 crossed her mind, one about Egyptian soldiers in such a hurry to run away that they left their boots behind.

She remembers that Doron was there, and it was the last time she saw him. There was a dogfight over the base when the two Phantoms returned. Then there were a few hours of quiet in this corner of Sinai as the day's disaster played out elsewhere. In the midst of it all, no one heard the Book of Jonah or the "Locking" prayer that concludes the Day of Atonement at sundown. That year it was as if the day never ended, as if it lasted for the next three weeks, or longer.

Up at the radar station the girls sat on the floor of one of the huts, filling ammunition clips. The windows were blacked out with Bristol board. Everyone knew the radar stations would be among the first targets in any war, and there were rumours that Egyptian helicopters had already dropped commandos in the desert nearby. They could arrive at any minute. The boys had been issued helmets and rifles, even though they weren't combat soldiers and weren't much more war-ready than the girls. They were posted around the rim of the hilltop in the sandbagged emplacements that they'd used until now for cigarette breaks. After dark, Pnina, the senior girl, went around and gave out slices of a cheesecake she'd brought from home. The last slices went to three of her friends sharing an emplacement, one of them black-haired Doron.

Orly had just finished a shift on the screens, with no time or inclination to copy any poetry on the Perspex, and was outside when she saw the sun flying toward her—that was her first thought, that the sun was shooting out of the night sky over the Red Sea. There was a flash when the missile hit, and the hill shook. She ran in the light of burning huts until she saw some of the others huddled under a camouflage net. Someone said to cover her head with her hands. A second missile hit the station. There was no air raid bunker to hide in, no shelter at all. The power went out. Suddenly they weren't electric youth with blow-dried hair overlooking the world from their clifftop, and they weren't soldiers of any invincible army. They were alone and helpless on this broken hill. Someone took a fire extinguisher and tried to put out the generators. Someone else said the two boys who'd been in the radio hut were dead, and it didn't seem possible, but one of the girls started screaming because her boyfriend was in there. The three boys who'd shared a guard post, the ones who'd eaten the last slice of cheesecake, couldn't be found. One of the girls started digging in the hard soil with her hands, as if she could tunnel her way to somewhere safe.

People down at the airfield saw the explosion. All the radios were dead. The hill just went black and stopped answering. The reports said the radar station and its soldiers had been captured by Egyptian commandos, and these reports were followed quickly by rumours that all of the surviving girls had been raped. It wasn't clear how anyone knew, but that's how rumours work in the army—they make explicit your worst fears.

In the middle of that night, the first of the war, twelve soldiers in three tanks were sent to recapture the radar station. The tanks happened to be of Soviet manufacture, a detail that turned out to matter; they'd been captured in the last war and painted with Israeli insignia. The tanks rumbled up the switchback road, the crews heading into battle for the first time. When the lead tank drew close to the gate, the gunner saw two soldiers. He opened fire and watched them fall.

Orly and Pnina, clustered with the others inside the damaged station, heard the enemy come roaring and clanking up the hill. The round turrets of Soviet tanks came into view and opened fire. The two Israelis guarding the gate dropped and lay still.

The tanks moved into the station and fired into the dining hut. One of the boys, Danny, was hit by shrapnel, and another, Judah, was gripping an old machine gun on a tripod, not that any of the radar technicians really knew what to do with a machine gun, and not that it was going to help against tanks. Pnina was in a trench a few yards away from the tanks, close enough to see the enemy commander with his head out of the hatch, close enough to hear him speak into his radio: "Aleph 1 to Aleph 2, over." The Egyptian was speaking Hebrew.

The station commander was already running toward the tanks waving a white shirt. Pnina got up too. She remembers the bewildered tank commander, who was not an Egyptian but an Israeli kid her age from a kibbutz in the north, staring at her from underneath his wide-eared helmet. He said, "There are girls here?" They all stood there looking at each other.

Ruti, at her telephone switchboard down at the airfield, knew something terrible had happened at the radar station— an attack and then a mistake. The Egyptians had rocketed the station but no enemy soldiers set foot there. The only ground combat that night was between Israelis. The soldiers didn't talk about it and wouldn't for thirty years. In those first days of the war there was enough bad news from elsewhere to pre-occupy them. The silver tail of a MiG-17 lay in the desert near Ruti's barracks, where it had fallen in the dogfight in the first minutes of the war. The body of the Egyptian pilot also lay there until someone took it away. Doron's mother and sister kept calling the switchboard to ask where he was, and Ruti said he wasn't around right now, but she'd pass on the message. That's what they had told her to say.

2

THE GATE OF HEAVEN

Leonard Cohen was on the island of Hydra, where he had a refuge in a little white house up the hill from the ferry dock. He'd happened upon the island a decade earlier, after he fled London, which is where he'd gone to flee Montreal. "A large part of my life was escaping. Whatever it was," he said later. "Even if the situation looked good, I had to escape, because it didn't look good to me. There was a selfish line in that, but it didn't seem so at the time, it just seemed a matter of survival."

He was introduced to the island by a few compelling bohemians who got there before him and was drawn by the cheap living, the donkeys and poverty and dazzling light—the opposite of the crushing concrete skies of the Canadian winters, the patches of dirty snow that blanket the frozen grass for half the year. "I'd never been in a sunny place and I'd never known what the sun was," he said, "so I fell in love with the sun, and a blond girl, and a white house." The girl was Marianne Ihlen, about whom he wrote a few songs that everybody knows, like "So Long, Marianne" and "Hey, That's No Way to Say Goodbye."

Cohen wrote the novel *Beautiful Losers* on the island, typing shirtless in the sun on speed, acid, and Quaaludes. Critics praised it, and there are still people who love it, but almost no one bought it at the time. He was on and off Hydra in the years of his rise from the small pond of Canadian letters into the Manhattan music world of Joan Baez and Nico and the Chelsea Hotel, where he was part of the scene but above it, in a suit when everyone was in jeans, someone who was bleak and funny and up to something else, and who evolved into a singular figure as the sixties wore on and wore thin.

By the fall of 1973 Cohen had drifted out of Marianne's life as he'd drifted out of many others. Now he was on the island with a baby, his first son, Adam, and with a dark-haired woman named Suzanne—not Suzanne of the song "Suzanne," who was a dancer he'd once known in Montreal, but a different Suzanne, who he'd met in New York. They weren't married in the legal sense, but she was Adam's mother, and he described her in writing as his wife. He was almost forty and no longer travelling light.

———

If this story has two magnetic poles, and the first is the Sinai desert, then the other is the Gate of Heaven, even though none of the story happens there. The Gate is five thousand miles west of Hydra, in Canada, over a continent and an ocean. If you're driving from Toronto, take Highway 401 east into the great flat country along the St. Lawrence, past the town of Napanee and a Shorelines Casino, past stretches of swamp, stands of oak, and summer homes, past the terminus of English Canada at the gas station outside Bainsville, into Quebec at the Esso Couche-Tard, and by the neat industrial parks of Vaudreuil-Dorion that announce the approaches to Montreal. Climb Mount Royal toward the fierce Catholic cross on the hilltop. You might think that's the Gate of Heaven—the people who put it up probably did—but it's not the one we're looking for.

The streets become more refined with altitude. This is Westmount. Find another cross, smaller and more polite, which the Anglicans put atop their heap of aspirational English stone at the Church of St. Matthias, then cross the street to a genteel fortress ringed with greenery. Every brick here suggests stability. Nothing hints that the building might be anything as wild as a portal to the divine—nothing but the discreet Hebrew letters identifying it as precisely that: Sha'ar Hashomayim. People here just call it the Sha'ar, the Gate.

The cornerstone of the Gate of Heaven came all the way from the land of Israel to be laid here in 1921 by Lyon Cohen. Lyon was the father of Nathan Cohen, who returned from World War I and married Masha, the daughter of a rabbi of genius from Kovno, Lithuania. The Cohens were descended from Temple priests, as their name denotes, and were leaders of the congregation. When Nathan's son was thirteen he was called to the Torah in this building as Eliezer ha-Cohen—Eliezer the Priest—but his English name was Leonard.

There are synagogues where dishevelled men and women scream out the prayers on the Day of Atonement, fingers rigid and pointing to the ceiling, prayer shawls and kerchiefs askew, the fast weakening their bodies, spurring panic and repentance over the many failures of the past year. This isn't that kind of synagogue. Here it's lowered voices and Louboutin. This kind of place preserves the tradition in wax, sealing its untamed core, which is a transmission to a tribe of slaves from a ferocious deity leading them out of Egypt through the wastes of Sinai, incarnated as a pillar of smoke before their camp, imparting death and life and knowledge, raising them up with glimpses of Himself, smashing them down with marauders and plague, drawing water from rocks. In Westmount you can't even imagine Sinai.

In 1964, when he was still just a Canadian poet, Cohen enraged listeners in Montreal with a speech dismissing the tidy edifice of the Jewish community's life as a hollow perversion of their divine mission. "We cannot face heaven," he said, the contempt in his voice audible in the old recording. "We have lost our genius for the vertical. Jewish novelists are sociologists. Horizontalists. And the residue of energy left from that great vertical seizure we had four thousand years ago—that we turn toward ourselves. We knock on our own doors and wonder that no one answers." What was needed now, he inveighed, wasn't priests but prophets, "dirty saints," "monstrous hermits." He called for "a moratorium on all religious services until someone reports a vision or breaks his mind on the infinite." That was one reason that when Yom Kippur arrived in 1973, the synagogue's most famous son wasn't there. He hadn't followed his father and uncles into the community leadership or the garment business. He was somewhere far away in the Mediterranean.

Cohen was stalked by depression for much of his life, and the months on Hydra before the war seem to have been dark. "I live here with a woman and a child," he wrote. "The situation makes me kind of nervous." An island is a place to escape to, but also a place where you're stranded. This mood is expressed in his written account of the journey to Sinai, the beginning of which appears in the next chapter. The writing is often livid and obscene. The way he writes about women, and the way he related to them, was part of the style of those days but is out of step with our own times. It might come as a shock to those unfamiliar with his earlier poetry and novels—who know his transcendent hits without knowing what he was transcending, or whose memories of the man come from his last incarnation as a gentleman in a suit. This later version of Cohen quipped that the first time he really met a woman was when he was sixty-five. The poet at thirty-nine, the one who travelled to Sinai and who typed this manuscript, is in the grip of anger and urges. He's trying to lose himself with women and drugs. He's a harder character to love.

That fall he felt frustrated, perhaps even trapped, not just by his new family and by middle age, but by his music. There had been a tour through Europe the year before, including two dates in Israel, that he thought went badly. The sublime moments he strived for eluded him onstage. He was disgusted by the music business and what it had done to him. "Once, long ago, my songs were not sold; they found their way to people anyway," he told an interviewer in March 1973. "Then people saw that profit could be made from them; then the profit interested me also."

He started saying he was retiring. "It's over," Cohen said that same year in an interview with Roy Hollingworth of *Melody Maker*. "I wish everybody well on 'the rock scene,' and may their music be great. May there be some good song-writers—and there will. But I don't want to be in it. I have songs in the air, but I don't know how to put them down. Anyway, I'm going." He went back to Hydra, and that's where things stood at the beginning of October, on Yom Kippur.

3

EGYPT'S BULLET

From Cohen's Lost Manuscript

I was listening to the war between the Arabs and the Jews. I wanted to go fight and die because she was so ugly to live with. My shoulder was bad either from helping the mason carry stones or gritting my teeth or both. Gritting my teeth from looking at the wreck of beauty and living inside of hatred and keeping to my side of the bed and always screaming no this can't be my life inside my head. I listened to the news every hour. I couldn't move. The war went on. Where was our miracle?*

---

* This is the manuscript Cohen typed on Hydra shortly after his return, published here for the first time. The entire document is too long to print in full, and parts aren't relevant to this story, so I've taken the liberty—with great trepidation—of abridging the text to distill the narrative of his journey to Sinai. I've corrected a few grammatical glitches and altered some of the spacing for clarity.

I heard myself talking to Anthony. I was talking about the Jewish Heart. We were on either side of a small table on the terrace. He was talking about the World Heart. I was talking about Jerusalem of Flesh and Stone. He was talking about Jerusalem of the Mind. It was a sunny morning in October. We were drinking Ovomaltine at a small wicker table I had brought from Athens long ago.

I said we live in a finite world. At least we live in a double world. We do not dwell in the realms of air. In this world the spirit is anchored in the mud. Jerusalem is not only a Christian hymn. It is the Capital of the Refugees. Is it really? Is it really?

One of us was talking. Our wives brought us Ovomaltine. The drink of meta-physicians. I said I'm only arguing to prolong this pleasant conversation. I know what I'm going to do.

He said it's easier to go than it is to stay. The excitement of war against this ordeal of warmth and monotony. Going is the easy way. Going is an alibi. We're not meant for the easy way.

I'm going I said.

I'm going too he said.

The landscape he said.

The war I said.

Whatever you say.*

---

* The character of Anthony serves an obvious literary purpose: he's the voice of universalism, a believer in the "world heart" as opposed to Cohen's "Jewish heart," skeptical of the poet's pull toward the state of Israel. But the reference is almost certainly to a real person, Anthony Kingsmill (1926–93), a British painter with whom Cohen was close on Hydra. Despite Anthony's stated intention to come along, perhaps drawn by a desire to paint "the landscape," he didn't.

My wife, what rays and wires and ethers connect us. What ribbons and trajectories, bold and fine as air routes, leaping in clean arcs over regions, moods, languages, one end sunk into your chest, one end into mine. What channels of intense air trembling to a signal. Like eyes aimed at stars, like the alloy of eyesight and starlight. What missions of spirit sperm rush through the glass air toward the lunar egg enthroned within your skeleton, all shadows and here is the shadow brood of hatred, love, remorse.

A dog is barking urgently on the black mountain. Perhaps you can hear him in your sleep. A black, slug-like insect came down the wall as I tried again to get back home. A bell has begun to ring. According to some religious schedule it must be the end of the night.

Whatever you say.

Put on the radio. Light up a cigarette. You are a normal citizen, after all. Fiddle among the stations. Find a good tune. Not the opera. Not the static. Not the passionate Arab violins. Not the armour-plated symphony. Not the shy French rhymer of birds and boats.* Turn off the radio. You can hear the wind again. Light up another cigarette. Lean forward. You're grown up. Jiggle your knees. Your penis isn't giving you any trouble. You are not aching with desire. Try the radio. The Greek is alright. It's midnight now. The governments are speaking. Try the silence again. Your government is speaking.

---

* A reference, perhaps, to Michel Polnareff's 1969 hit "Tous les bateaux, tous les oiseaux," or "All the boats, all the birds."

It won't resign.* It won't vomit. It won't wake up your wife and bring her smiling into the room all warm to say, I had a dream. We were married under a wave. The child is awake.

Turn on the radio. They are actually playing Deutschland Uber Alles. Someone who sounds like Dylan. Italian news. Glenn Miller on the Voice of America.

I said, Because it is so horrible between us I will go and stop Egypt's bullet. Trumpets and a curtain of razorblades. Organ music.

She said, that's beautiful. Then I can commit suicide and the child falls into strangers' hands.

What you did to me, she said.

What you did to me, I said.

The lonely, we said. The nights of hands on ourselves. Your unkindness, we said. Your greed. Your unkindness. Your bitter tongue. Give me time. You never learn. Your ancestors. My ancestors. Fuck you, I said. You shit. Stop screaming. I can't stand it. You can't stand anything. Nobody can live like this. In front of the child. Let him learn. This is no good. Yer fuckn right it's no good.

This kitchen was once beautiful. Oil lamps, order, the set table. Sabbath observed. That's what I want. You don't want it. You don't know what I want. You don't know anything about me. You never did. Not in the beginning. Not now. In the realms where this marriage was sealed, where the wedding feast goes on and on, where Adam and Eve face one another, the foundations are faultless and secure, your

* In Washington, DC, the Watergate scandal was at its height.

beast hair flares like black fire upward and your breasts, now in maidenhood, now in motherhood, drawn down my face, our hunger blessed by sun and moon, a ring of dancers round the house where within the room is hid, where within the bed is undone, whereupon the hunger's joined, where within the one speaks himself expressions yet unknown.

I'll be on my way.

I went down to the port with my wife. On the way down I accused her of continuing her relentless automatic assault on the centre of my being. I knew this was not wise. I meant only to rap her on the knuckles and direct her attention to her habitual drift toward bitchiness but I lost control. There is no control in these realms. I became a thug. I attacked her spirit. Her spirit armed itself and retaliated massively. I'm glad you didn't pack for me. You always slow me down. I can't be an acrobat when you're around.

The shoemaker looked up at us as we passed his open doorway. This humiliation made me furious. I shoved a razor blade into her nerves. Her eyes changed colour. This was done by saying Jesus Christ, quickening my step slightly, minutely moving my jaw, rejecting the essence of her totally and forever. Half-asleep Old John saw us but it was no humiliation since he didn't recognize me anymore and I no longer greeted him. Captain Mad Body saw us but it didn't matter because he was mute and crazy and lived on the port and knew the shames of everyone. We were on the port, in plain sunlight between the masts and the shops. The horn, the boat was coming. I would have to travel without your blessing in the collapsed world. That's the boat.

The *Naeraia* came in, its white decks above us. I know the name of a boat or two. Ropes were flying, uniforms flashing, everywhere haste advised and the threat of lost time. I stared at her as she became beautiful and calm. I would not get the blessing. The journey had an unclean start.

Once on the boat I was on the boat. I didn't climb the upper deck to wave goodbye to one whose blessings were unconfirmed. She must take her dead blessings up the hill back to the house. When she got home she pinned a blue ribbon to the inside of my windbreaker, next to where the heart would be. She showed me this much later. Certainly a factor in my coming back alive.

I sat down next to a man who had done some work. There are always such people around to illumine one's sloth. The modesty of this one was especially reproachful. His hands told me how lazy I am. His quietness told me how loud. His wrinkles told me how weak I am. His shoulders told me how proud.

We came to the island of Aigina, home of the pistachio nut, last stop before Piraeus. Anthony said that George said that at first you only want to look at the front of them but after a while you only want to see them from behind.

Stamatis boarded the ship at Aigina, a cunt-struck land-owner from this very island. I asked him if he had any news of Lizette, an English inn-keeper of mutual acquaintance who had a sad reputation of biting into cocks, disinterested information of her existence being the mainstay of our accidental annual conversations. Yes, he had news, but not very pleasant news. She had come to Athens. She had contacted him.

They had arranged a rendezvous but both turned up at different times due to a misunderstanding of clocks. Some time later when he called her hotel he was informed that she was not able to use the telephone. He summoned the hotel manager to the line and he was advised not to come to the hotel, it was not a pretty sight. Some weeks later he received a letter from Lizette, postmarked London, with a characteristically depressing explanation. Apparently she had been badly tortured by three Japanese tourists behind a restaurant. This was the first conversation I had enjoyed with Stamatis in a long time. Do you believe this preposterous story? I said to him.

It was amazing how clear-brained and happy I had become. Just a little sea between me and the creature of unbeauty and the world had begun to come alive. He stuffed a cigarette into an ivory tube and pretended not to hear me. We sipped our ouzos, perfectly content, giving nothing, two men of the world.

-Why aren't you in Israel, he said, thinking he had me there.

-As a matter of fact, that's exactly where I'm going.

-Really? Really? He stood up, delighted.

-I'll go directly to the airport as soon as we dock. That's what I'm doing here.

-Bravo, he said. Really. Bravo. Bravo. Bravo. Oh I'm so pleased. Bravo. Bravo. Bravo. Bravo. He seized both my hands in his and squeezed them with true enthusiasm

and something like gratitude. Evidently I now represented certain old virtues which he cherished deeply.
More than love of cunt did we share together. We were
the shield, the men who defended. My house, his house.
My land, his land. Because of this we were granted
cigarette holders, loneliness, and the right to speak of
women casually.

-You must. You must, he said.

-I know. I felt humble and doomed. His eyes seemed to
be shining at an honoured corpse. The degree of his
admiration had attracted more than several of our fellow
passengers. These he commenced to address in Greek
as follows:

-This man is travelling to Israel to defend his country
against his country's enemy. He leaves a well-appointed
house, a woman and a child, all the comforts of his
achievement. I wonder how many of you, if you lived
let us say in Holland or Sweden in similar circumstances,
would sacrifice your security and come back here, if the
threat arose, to fight against the Turk. Bravo, Leonard.
Bravo. Bravo. Bravo. With a contemptuous wave of the
hand he sent his audience back to their private chamber
to reconsider their cowardice, and we embraced. I must
be doing something really stupid, I said to myself, to
make another man so happy.

4

ACCORDING TO WHOSE PLAN?

It wasn't easy to reach Israel in the first days of the war, not just because of flight disruptions but because thousands of people across the world were trying to get there, besieging the El Al counters at Heathrow and Orly. Many were young Israelis trying to join their reserve units, like Isaac in Tokyo and Shlomi in London, who appear here later on. The airline had priority lists from the army, and at first you weren't allowed on a plane if you couldn't serve in a tank or a hospital, which was a sign of how things were going. Some of the people at the airports were civilians desperate to get back to their families in Israel. Some weren't even Israelis. In Florida, for example, a Jewish eye doctor heard the news in synagogue on Yom Kippur and was on a plane with his operating instruments the same day. Another American doctor was operating on soldiers four hours after landing from Pittsburgh. A surgeon from Cape Town, South Africa, pushed onto a flight, landed at Lod, and was sent directly to the front in Sinai.

In those days a distress call from Israel affected some like the Bat Signal of the comics, or Susan's horn in Narnia. It might seem hard to understand now. It was even then. Many of the people who responded surprised themselves, like my father, who was a graduate student in Toronto in June 1967 when war broke out between Israel and Egypt, Jordan, and Syria. Like many Jews who grew up in the West after World War II, he had little to do with Jewish ritual and couldn't speak Hebrew. If Jews in Israel had staked their futures on citizenship in an embattled Jewish state, my father and his peers were counting on the goodwill of a majority that seemed open to having them. Wars in the Middle East were not part of his life. But in June 1967 he found himself calling the Israeli consulate in Toronto to ask how he could fly over to help this country where he'd never been and where he didn't know a soul. They thanked him and said he wasn't urgently needed.

Another person with the same idea was the fiery, dissolute Montreal poet Irving Layton, one of Cohen's mentors and closest friends. Layton was born Israel Lazarovitch and changed his name, as many did, but not his allegiances. Aviva Layton, the poet's partner for two decades and the mother of his son, remembered him heading off to the Israeli consulate in 1967 to volunteer for the army at age fifty-five, coming back crestfallen that they wouldn't take him. "At that time," Aviva said, "before we had any political stances about Israel one way or another, it was just an atavistic Jewish thing."

The sentiment might belong to an older generation, and to a time when Israel was more vulnerable. But it shows up as recently as 2016 in Jonathan Safran Foer's novel *Here I Am*, in which an American-Jewish family falls apart as Israel is struck by catastrophe and invaded. The main character gathers his courage and surprises himself by heading off to the war. Entering a Long Island airport to be vetted by the Israelis, he finds other volunteers singing "Jerusalem of Gold," a patriotic song from the 1967 war that Jewish kids learn at summer camp. "I had written books and screenplays my entire life," the character reflects, "but it was the first time I'd felt like a character inside one—that the scale of my tchotchke existence, the *drama* of living, finally befitted the privilege of being alive."

Cohen was born in 1934, so he remembered World War II and what it meant not to have a Jewish state. Israel was created in 1948, when he was fourteen. In 1961, when Cohen was twenty-seven and Israel was thirteen, he'd addressed the country in "Lines from My Grandfather's Journal," which appears in his second book of poems. The grandfather is his mother's father, Rabbi Solomon Klonitzki-Kline of Kovno. Having escaped Europe for the new world, and witnessed the fates of those not as lucky, the old rabbi—in the words of his Canadian grandson—considers this twist in Jewish history:

Soldiers in close formation. Paratroops in a white Tel Aviv street. Who dares disdain an answer to the ovens? Any answer.

I did not like to see the young men stunted in the Polish ghetto. Their curved backs were not beautiful. Forgive me, it gives me no pleasure to see them in uniform. I do not thrill to the sight of Jewish battalions.

But there is only one choice between ghettos and battalions, between whips and the weariest patriotic arrogance . . .

One early expression of Cohen's take on war and communal allegiance appears in his protest song "Story of Isaac," which he wrote four years before the events that interest us, at the height of the war in Vietnam. The text is based on the story from Genesis about how Abraham was willing to sacrifice his son because God told him to. It ends,

> And if you call me Brother now,
> forgive me if I enquire:
> Just according to whose plan?
> When it all comes down to dust
> I will kill you if I must,
> I will help you if I can.
> When it all comes down to dust
> I will help you if I must,
> I will kill you if I can.
> And mercy on our uniform,
> man of peace, man of war—
> the peacock spreads his fan!

The song, which is blunter and more topical than Cohen usually allowed himself to be, includes the lines "You who build these altars now / To sacrifice these children / You must not do it anymore," but Cohen wasn't a pacifist. One of his most enduring songs remained his rendition of "The Partisan," an ode to armed resistance, while "Story of Isaac"

41

eventually dropped off the setlist. He didn't want to be confused with John Lennon. "I don't have to have a song called 'Give Peace a Chance,'" he said in an interview seven months before the Yom Kippur War. "I could write a song about conflict and, if I sang it in a peaceful way, then it would have the same message. I don't like these slogan writers."

Neither did Cohen believe in the world of Lennon's "Imagine," where people live without nation or religion. Cohen took an interest in Eastern spirituality, using the I Ching a lot in those days, and eventually spending years in a Buddhist monastery, Mt. Baldy in California. But he never thought he'd turned his back on his origins. "A lot of people who think that I've changed my religion look very suspiciously or even scornfully or even express great disappointment that I've abandoned my own culture, that I've abandoned Judaism," he told a Swedish interviewer at the monastery in 1997. "Well, I was never looking for a new religion. I have a very good religion, which is called Judaism. I have no interest in acquiring another religion."

He once responded with scorn to his fellow Montrealer, the writer Mordecai Richler, who'd rejected the Jewish community and the country that produced him and suggested in 1964 that Canada dissolve itself into the United States. Cohen thought the only culture worth anything came from loyalty to a language, a group, a place, and that a world without those differences would be unbearable. "Only nationalism produces art," he said. He thought Judaism and Canada were worth preserving, and indeed that they had a few things in common. "The Canadians are like the Jews—they're constantly examining their identity," he said. "We're on the edge of a great empire, and this throws the whole thing into a very special kind of relief." Cohen didn't let his loyalties define him. But he maintained them.

Armed with this complicated set of attachments, and escaping attachments that were more personal and possibly more complicated, he arrived alone at Ellinikon International Airport in Athens, en route to Tel Aviv.

5

A WOUND IN THE JEWISH WAR

From Cohen's Lost Manuscript

The airport. A description of the airport. Yes, I recognize this. It's an airport. How pleasant to recognize it from mere words. How real it is, the marble, the neon, the bad ball pens. Or is this the bank? No, it's the airport.

There was one seat left on the plane to Tel Aviv. Nothing can stop me. My luck has changed. The girls in uniform smile at my airport style. I hate to leave them all behind. This man's travelling. I am thin again and loose. I suntan myself from within.

I cruised the racks of cards and books. I bought an envelope and filled it with all the drachmas I had in my pocket and mailed it back to the island with a note which began Dearest One. Without her blessing my freedom was precarious.

I had seen a man and a man had seen me. I had seen him move to watch me. He was young, thin, moustached, lightfooted, grey-suited, nor did his business seem to be flying.

I had seen him watching carefully as I sat on the marble floor in a marble corner waiting for flight news. I supposed I was too old to be sitting on the floor and my leather bag which I sat beside in a most friendly manner was altogether too old. My bag was the nearest thing I had to a dog. I might have been patting it.

Now as I left the airport post office he intercepted me. He was very light-footed and I was not so much stopped as my movement diverted. He showed me something in his wallet and politely explained, Security. Please follow me. I followed him, not to an office as I expected, but into a Men's Room, the nearest public Men's Room. I said to myself, This is the fine edge of a humiliation.

We stopped at the sinks. The mirrors were bright. One policeman was shaving. At the urinals another policeman was pissing. There were no civilians in this Men's Room. I hope I don't have to undress. I hope my courage is not tested.

-Passport.

-*Amessos*.

-How is it you speak Greek?

-I live here. I am a Greek-lover.

Must we endure this tedious anecdote? It illumines nothing. It merely happened. Your organ was not smashed across the porcelain with a billy-club. We who have observed the extraction of ten fingernails resent these luxuries.

-Why are you leaving us, O Greek-lover?

We terminate this anecdote as of now. Although it is well-meaning and not deliberately false, it is already too inaccurate and flat to be of any value to either the reader or the writer.

-I'm going to Israel. The war.

We were waiting to be searched before boarding the aircraft. I could see that certain people had recognized me. No one I wanted to fuck but some I wanted to look at naked, especially a girl whose eyes are looking at me now, suddenly she's so kind and lovely.

Their names are Asher and Margolit. They are standing in front of me in the line. We introduced ourselves. They said they knew who I was. Get me out of here. He was earnest, bearded, muscular, excited, blue fanatic eyes. He surprised me by saying, I'd like to be your friend, if it's possible. Shit, I have to take this man seriously. The cities are blacked out, it's hard to get around, would I like to stay with them that night? Thank you. Let my seats be far from them so I can sit alone. No pressure coming from Margolit. She is counting time by her own slow clock.

-Did you tell him your other name? Margolit asked him.

-No. I told him the only name I have.

The story is that Asher is American, a convert to Judaism, a citizen of Israel, circumcised last year. So he had his wound in the Jewish war, he had paid in adult sin and blood to be numbered among us. It was in his jeans but he carried the mutilation across his shoulder like a duffel-bag, and peeking over his load of suffering was the crazy grin of a Jesus freak, a California mystic screaming, God is our History. These are people who believe in words. Should we have let them look at our Bible? People like me wrote the Bible. We did it out of malice and despair.

We land in Tel Aviv, Asher checks in at the military desk and shows them his deferment. He has diabetes. I am in my myth home but I have no proof and I cannot debate and I am in no danger of believing myself. We wait for a friend's car. It is very dark. All the headlights are painted blue. Speaking no Hebrew I enjoy my legitimate silence. We drove slowly on the darkened highways listening to news of the war on the radio. I didn't ask them to interpret the solemn voices. I have homes here and there, I never understand the languages where I have my homes.

It was two in the morning when we came to the house of Margolit's parents in Herzliya, a suburb of Tel Aviv. That was Judith's window, her younger sister. Oh there is a younger sister. We threw pebbles at the window.

I stand up in the morning and I give praise to the lord who has delivered sunlight into the world and the beams of his star against my skin. I am the army of a thousand men but he is one forever and forever. Here I am, dear father. You pour out my heart into your world. The snow in Montreal.

We threw pebbles at her window, or did we call up? I never lie to you.

Judith came down and opened the door. Please let me into her nightgown. Her mother woke up, a tall handsome jewess from Finland. We sat around the dining-room table waiting for the water to boil. Judith's dressing-gown parted for an instant and her warm sleepy thighs sent forth a lonely feast all laid for no one, and drew a curtain over it with a gesture of automatic modesty.

We travellers had come looking for the war, an airplane filled with us. Judith and her mother didn't know where the war was. They had tried to volunteer for things but all they had managed to do was plant flowers on a kibbutz a few afternoons ago. It was rather disturbing feeling so untouched by it, and listening to sad news on the radio every hour. They still went to the beach every day. The war was somewhere else.

-Did you come to sing for the troops? they asked.

-No, I came to gobble up the younger sister.

-I didn't think so, Asher said. He thought I had come for the same reasons as he and Margolit. To be there. Not to stand idly by our brother's blood. Perhaps to recover from the vanities of the singing profession. It is becoming clear that neither the night nor the family will marry

me and Judith in the guestroom or behind the house
or meeting accidentally on the way to the bathroom.
I guess I'll say goodnight. Thank you for the hospitality.
Myself, I do not like male strangers in the house, but you
are obviously on a higher spiritual rung than me. I notice
that Asher refers to God from time to time. He has indications of what God wants us to do. All of us look at him
strangely as if to say, This lunatic seems to be taking it
all seriously.

Directions to the bus stop. Waiting alone for the bus.
The first moment without people. Just me and my brown
leather bag. The independent observer.

I checked into the Gad Hotel after a bus ride along the
sea during which I blessed myself for being alone and not
with you.* The Gad Hotel is bed for soldiers and hookers,
Hayarkon Street near Frischman. I was given room eight.

Now Aleece was present in the small office when I signed
my name and gave my number. I did not know what her
function was but I knew she was connected to the hotel.
There was something absent and mechanical in her presence. [She had] stainless steel legs. They were extremely
tall, shapely but austere and muscular, and they soared
above her spikes like the steel scaffolding of a bridge. She
was a sexual construction. I have touched her holes and
looked into her clear blue eyes of panic and I am not certain

---

* It's not entirely clear to whom Cohen's occasional slips into the
second person are addressed, though Suzanne is the likeliest candidate.

she is not a robot. Her hair was blond and perfect but too thin, as if she had neglected to renew it at the inventor's. She said she was from Amsterdam, but her speech was not perfected and she spoke no language very well. She was the one before the inventor's masterpiece, when his energy was lust, and he was still trying to establish in the gross world his ideal sexual fantasy. This is a strange flower in a small hotel.

I climbed the stairs with the key and my brown leather bag and I entered room eight.* I heard Aleece mounting the steps behind me. Room eight. My own room in a warm country. A bed, a table, a chair. Perhaps I could become a poet again. Aleece was making noises in the hall. I could see the ocean in the late afternoon outside the window. I should look at the ocean but I don't feel like it. The interior voice said, you will only sing again if you give up lechery. Choose. This is a place where you may begin again. But I want her, wuf, wuf. Please let me have her. Throw yourself upon your stiffness and take up your felt pen.

---

* Like the Greek landowner Cohen meets on the ship in the previous section, Aleece is a character familiar to readers of *Death of a Lady's Man*, where a version of this episode appears. It's as if the parts of the manuscript that seem the tawdriest, and which reflect most poorly on him, were the ones Cohen wanted to publish.

She makes noise in the hallway
Come in
She comes in
Out to the balcony
Stand behind her
Say, Lean over
Up with her skirt
Drool in my hand
to open it up
Watch the sunset
over her hair
Are you connected
to the hotel the chambermaid
No, I'm the one
you are writing about
the one who sails down
the pillars of blood
from brain to isthmus
and lost in your unhanded trousers
I cause myself to come true

How noble I felt after writing these lines. Aleece had gone away. The emanations of my labor had cleared the hallway.

6

MYTH HOME

Tel Aviv then wasn't what is now. It wasn't wealthy or international. It was a small Mediterranean city founded just sixty-four years earlier, with some crumbling old buildings that were lovely before the humidity and salt got at them, and new ones that were ugly from the start. Nearly everyone over thirty who lived there had escaped from Europe or the Arab world, and many of them screamed in their sleep. But the city had a good beach and some bohemian energy. The writers and artists hung out at a café called Casit, at another called California, and at Café Pinati, five blocks from Cohen's hotel.

Cohen had been in the city before. His introduction to the Israeli audience had occurred there a year and a half earlier, in April 1972, when he played a sports hall at the end of that year's troubled European tour. He was accompanied by a band he called the Army, which included Bob Johnston, the legendary producer of Dylan and Johnny Cash, roped in as keyboard player; the guitarist Ron Cornelius, with sunglasses and droopy moustache; and the backup singers Jennifer Warnes and Donna Washburn, in gypsy skirts and shawls. The chaos was caught on film by a crew shooting a tour documentary that Cohen ended up hating and wouldn't release.

The floor by the stage had been cleared to protect new polyurethane applied to the basketball court, keeping the fans an absurd distance from the performers. Cohen—his eyes unfocused and his voice slurred, hints of the chemicals that fuelled that tour—invited everyone to move closer. They surged toward him, but orange-shirted guards began pushing them back, then using their fists, and the concert spun out of control. Cohen implored the guards to stop and tried to keep singing but had to give up. "There's no point in starting a war right now," he said and left the stage with the rattled band.

Two days later in Jerusalem, the last concert of the 1972 tour almost became a worse debacle. The film shows Cohen taking acid in the dressing room before the show. The audience was rapt and there was no riot. This time it was Cohen's fault. He lost focus after a few songs and stopped the performance in the middle. The Army had been across Europe on the tour, and there had been some tough shows, like one in Berlin where Cohen taunted a rowdy audience with Nazi slogans, and a few where the sound equipment malfunctioned. But nothing like this had happened. There was something going on between the singer and the Jerusalem audience. "I felt this atmosphere once before," he said offstage afterward, trying to figure it out for himself. "It was in Montreal. My entire family was there."

Instead of singing, he started talking to the crowd about Jewish mysticism. "Some nights," he said, "one is raised off the ground, and some nights you just can't get off the ground. There's no point lying about it. And tonight we just haven't been getting off the ground. It says in the Kabbalah"—the ancient mystic text got a few cheers, because in Jerusalem that's like a hometown shout-out—"It says in the Kabbalah that if you can't get off the ground, you should stay on the ground. It says in the Kabbalah that unless Adam and Eve face each other, God does not sit on his throne. Somehow the male and the female parts of me refused to encounter one another tonight, and God does not sit on his throne. And this is a terrible thing to happen in Jerusalem." He walked off, and someone went out to offer everyone their money back.

Another crowd might have left or got angry. But instead the people in the auditorium starting singing "Hevenu Shalom Aleichem" (We've brought peace upon you). It's a basic song taught at every Hebrew school, just those three words over and over. Maybe they sensed this was something they had in common with Cohen—he was family, he must know the song! He did know the song. The young audience was from the age group that was going to be ground up in the war the following year. When you watch them, you wonder who among them won't see the end of 1973. They sang for a long time. Cohen heard it from his dressing room as he tried to calm down. Eventually he came back and just stood there for a while, beaming out at the people singing, like he couldn't believe it.

He sang "Hey, That's No Way to Say Goodbye" and "So Long, Marianne," and when the show finally ended, the audience still wouldn't go home. Cohen was crying, and the backup singers were embracing each other and crying—it's all in the film. The crowd was begging for more, but the band was overwhelmed and falling apart. Cohen went back out. "Hey, listen, people, my band and I are all crying backstage there," he said. "We're too broken up to go on, but I just wanted to tell you thank you, and good night." He walked off for the last time. "What an audience," he was saying. "Ever see anything like that?"

Many years later, he remembered the moment he went back onstage to sing "So Long, Marianne" under the combined weight of his own history, Jewish history, LSD, and Jerusalem, which isn't a place inclined to let you take it lightly. "I see Marianne straight in front of me and I started crying," he remembered. "I turned around and the band was crying, too. And then it turned into something in retrospect quite comic: the entire audience turned into one Jew! And this Jew was saying, 'What else can you show me, kid? I've seen a lot of things, and this don't move the dial!' And this was the entire skeptical side of our tradition, not just writ large but manifested as an actual gigantic being! Judging me hardly begins to describe the operation. It was a sense of invalidation and irrelevance that I felt was authentic, because those feelings have always circulated around my psyche: Where do you get to stand up and speak? For what and whom? And how deep is your experience? How significant is anything you have to say?"

That's how he put it forty-three years later. It may or may not have anything to do with what he thought at the time. But it does seem clear that Cohen's idea that this foreign country was his "myth home" made being here confusing. The relationship was powerful and tenuous, like being in love with someone you don't really know.

Back here the following year, alone this time, with no one expecting him and no concerts to play, and with the country gripped by dread, Cohen left the hotel and walked away from the beach, headed for a café he remembered, hoping to find a certain woman. At this point in his manuscript, the pace of events picks up and forces him out of the familiar and often squalid contours of his interior landscape. He gives up on crafting a narrative and instead starts making a list.

1. I changed my clothes.
2. I walked up Frischman to the Cafe Pinoti, where I looked for Rochel.*
3. I went back to the hotel and washed my shirt. I found a place to hang it on the balcony where it would not flap against the dirty walls.
4. I forced myself to look at the Sea for some moments, trying to convince myself of the salutary effects of this effort.
5. I went to bed and slept badly because of the mosquitoes.

---

* Cohen's archaic Hebrew pronunciation was the kind used by European Jews in synagogue, with the vowel "o" where modern Hebrew has "a"—hence "Pinoti" instead of Pinati, and "Rochel" for "Rachel."

6. I was so happy when it was the morning.
7. I went to the Cafe Pinoti, looking for Rochel.
    I decided not to look for her.
8. I took a bus to the beach at Herzlia. I was so happy
    in the water. I promised myself to be faithful. I
    decided to find a shack and live by myself on this
    beach, not telling anyone.
9. I went back to the hotel. After I had showered and
    changed I walked up Frischman to the empty Cafe
    Pinoti and up and down the black-out streets look-
    ing for Rochel.
10. I sprayed the room and went to sleep.
11. I woke up and got into the sunshine. It was too early
    to look for Rochel. I went to the Cafe Pinoti to drink
    coffee and read the *Herald Tribune*. Several people
    seemed to recognize me.
12. I met an Israeli singer, Ilana Rovina. She had just
    come back from the Sinai. She was singing that night
    at an Air Base and the next day she and three other
    entertainers were going back to the Sinai. Would I
    like to join them?

1. I changed my clothes.

2. I walked up Frischman to the Cafe Pinoti, where I looked for Rochel.

3. I went back to the Hotel and washed my shirt. I found a place to hang it on the balcony where it would not flap against the dirty walls.

4. I forced myself to look at the Sea for some moments, trying to convince myself of the salutary effects of this effort.

5. I went to bed and slept badly because of the mosquitoes.

6. I was so happy when it was the morning.

7. I went to the Cafe Pinoti, looking for ~~Frank~~ Rochel. I decided not to look for her.

8. I took a bus to the beach at Herzlia. I was so happy in the water. I promised myself to be faithful. I decided to find a shack and live by myself on this beach, not telling anyone.

9. I went back to the Hotel. After I had showered and changed I walked up Frischman to the empty Cafe Pinoti and up and down the black-out streets looking for Rochel.

10. I sprayed the room and went to sleep.

11. I woke up and got into the sunshine. It was too early to look for Rochel. I went to the Cafe Pinoti to drink coffee and read the Herald Tribune. Several people seemed to recognize me.

7

BEGINNING AGAIN

The woman he was looking for was Rachel Teri, a beautiful volleyball player and flight attendant from a Yemeni family. They had met the previous year at a party near Tel Aviv. Someone said Leonard Cohen would be there, she told a journalist years later, but she didn't know who that was. "Suddenly his manager came up to me and said Leonard wants to meet me," she recounted. "I said, 'Are you kidding?' The friend I came with said, 'Go, what's the big deal?' So I went with the manager, who brought me into a small room. Leonard was sitting there on the floor. There was a chair and he invited me to sit. Then he said, 'I just want you to tell me, yes or no.' That was all."

She said yes, and they were photographed a few times by the Israeli tabloids, which took an interest in Cohen and the people he knew. American celebrities showed up occasionally in those days: Dylan came quietly around the same time, and Leonard Bernstein came much less quietly, with a film crew. Tel Aviv was a backwater and any international star drew attention.

Cohen didn't find Rachel that day. But when he sat down at Café Pinati there was a good chance he'd be recognized. There are minor variations on the story of what happened next. In Cohen's account, the central character was the singer Ilana Rovina, the product of a scandalous affair three decades earlier between one of Israel's greatest actresses and one of its greatest poets. Cohen's manuscript doesn't mention anyone in the café except her, but she was with Oshik Levi, a shaggy-haired balladeer who was then at the height of his fame. After the Six-Day War, when the West was briefly in love with Israelis for its own complex and guilty reasons, Oshik had travelled as part of an Israeli folk music revue that packed halls in Europe and America. In Paris everyone who mattered came—Yves Montand, Charles Aznavour, Serge Gainsbourg. "At that time we were," Oshik told me, switching to English, "*de izraeli hero*." That's how he got to see the world. He'd grown up in an Israel where the stern socialist arbiters of taste were still in control. They wouldn't let the Beatles come because they might corrupt the youth. For years you had to tune into a Jordanian station, Radio Ramallah, to hear rock 'n' roll. So on the *izraeli hero* tour they'd sing the old folk music, which they wouldn't dream of listening to themselves anymore, and then he'd go off to see Hendrix or the Stones. He knew who Leonard Cohen was.

In Rovina's account of the meeting at the café, Oshik turned to her and said, "The guy sitting over there by himself looks like Leonard Cohen."

"You wish," she replied.

Oshik said, "I'm serious, it's Leonard Cohen," and went over to prove her wrong.

"We invited him to sit with us," Rovina remembered. "We said we were singers, and asked what he was doing in Israel. He said, 'I heard there's a war, so I came to volunteer for harvest work on the kibbutzim and to release a few guys to fight.' We told him there was no harvest right now, and suggested he come play concerts with us. He said he was a pacifist." Rovina was probably mistaken about Cohen describing himself that way, or she was using that word more generally to mean he was repelled by violence. Cohen never called himself a pacifist. In any case, she reassured him, "We aren't fighting, just playing music."

In Rovina's memory, two other people were also at the table. One was Matti Caspi, an introverted genius who is now considered one of Israel's best musicians, but who was then twenty-three and just beginning to make himself felt. The other was Pupik Arnon, a comic actor and occasional singer whose real name was Mordechai. As a short kid in high school he'd been stuck with the nickname Pupik, meaning "belly button." Pupik starred in some of the most popular Israeli movies of those years. He was, by his own account, perpetually high. When I met him he was an ultra-Orthodox rabbi. Pupik didn't remember being in the café for the first meeting with Cohen and thinks he and Matti Caspi joined afterward.

In Oshik's memory, he was in the café by himself. Customers were drinking coffee and eating croissants, he recalled, even though soldiers were dying a few hours' drive away. Tel Aviv has always been a bubble. Combat soldiers spoke of the city with contempt, and still do, while simultaneously dreaming of getting back there. Oshik remembered going over and introducing himself. Cohen said, "I heard you guys are in trouble, and I came to work on a kibbutz."

"I told him to come play music," Oshik remembered. Cohen replied, "Look, my songs are melancholy, 'Bird on the Wire' and so forth, I'll just get them depressed.' I said, 'It's fine, just come.'"

Whatever the precise cast of the meeting at the café, Cohen was inducted there into the improvised musical corps that has followed the Israeli army into battle since the Independence War of 1948. When fighting starts, the country's singers show up to play—it's considered part of being a successful musician, a kind of tax you pay for not fighting yourself. The art, the artists, and the army are all mixed up. Some singers were once combat soldiers themselves. Many, like Oshik and Pupik, had come up through the military entertainment troupes that were beloved of both soldiers and civilians. The military troupes provided much of Israel's upbeat, on-message, accordion-heavy soundtrack right up to 1973, when the war killed the genre, and the accordion.

One of the archetypes of this Israeli mix of the military and the musical came at the height of the 1948 war, when a composer in Tel Aviv wrote a tune for a song called "The Last Battle." The lyrics were by a poet who was serving in the war himself. The singer, Shoshana Damari, learned the tune between two performances at the Li-La-Lo Theatre, and after the second performance someone showed up breathlessly to tell her about a group of soldiers who were having a last meal at a nearby café before leaving to fight the Egyptian invasion force in the Negev desert. Could she sing for them? She ran over to the café and performed the new song, whose lyrics might be a premonition of doom or a hope for peace: "Who knows, sister, if we'll come back to you? Maybe this battle is the last . . ." The soldiers were headed for a place that became infamous as the Fallujah Pocket, and for seven of them it was the last battle.

As Cohen met his new friends at the café, dozens of musicians were already headed toward the front in helicopters and Hercules transports, in old buses, or in their private cars, like Oshik's Ford Falcon. After Cohen agreed to come along, he mentioned that he didn't have a guitar.

This odd detail raises a good question: What, exactly, did Cohen think he was going to do in Israel? If he didn't bring a guitar, it seems he didn't plan to perform. There's no reason to think he knew about the tradition of Israeli musicians following the troops. And at the time, as his public comments showed, he'd despaired of his songs and said he was retiring. He wanted to "shut up." That's probably why he came empty-handed, and without telling anyone. He didn't travel to Israel as Leonard Cohen the artist. He might not have been sure that's still who he was.

Cohen's manuscript about the war tends to raise more questions than it answers. He's unwilling to explain directly what he was thinking. There's the line about "stopping Egypt's bullet," which sounds heroic, and over the years there have been a few suggestions that he meant to fight. It's hard to take this seriously. Cohen wasn't foolish enough to think you could show up in a war, get a gun, and go off to stop a bullet. To the extent that he had a real plan, there's no reason to doubt what the musicians heard him say in the café, which is that he thought he'd work at a kibbutz. Many Western volunteers had done so in the 1967 war, replacing workers called up to the front.

The question of why he really came is different, and more consequential, than the question of what he thought he'd do. Here, too, Cohen gives us few clues. But there is an important one buried in his description of the encounter with Aleece at the hotel, when he's in Room 8 and she's outside the door, waiting to come in. "The interior voice said, you will only sing again if you give up lechery. Choose," he tells himself. "This is a place where you may begin again." This motivation seems even more genuine because it's not presented as a declaration of intent, with dramatic trumpets, but as an aside in a story about something else. Cohen wanted a way out of his dead end. We know that he didn't really give up in 1973. He was looking for a way to sing again and might have been seeking what he'd called a "vertical seizure," a revelation like one the Israelites had experienced long ago in Sinai. This was the place where he thought it could happen.

After the musicians left the café, one of them made a call to an air force officer. The air force was hemorrhaging planes and pilots at a rate so shocking it was being hidden from the public, but someone there still found time to get a guitar for Leonard Cohen. None of the artists had any idea how bad things were, or what they were getting themselves into. Cohen climbed into the Ford Falcon and went off to find the war.

8

WHO BY WATER

There were so many planes in the sky that they reminded one pilot of the huge Allied raids of World War II. The first wave was Skyhawks that flew over the dry hills of northern Israel, then over the blue oval of the Sea of Galilee and into the death zone above the Golan Heights.

From the ground it was tiny metal triangles passing overhead, a flitting shadow on your tank. Up in a Skyhawk you saw the dials, buttons, and lights, the cross of the sight, the oxygen tube. The plane had an ugly, efficient American cockpit, not like the French machines the air force used to fly, where you were raised high above the fuselage and saw the wings spread elegantly behind you. The pilots still liked to use French for airplane parts, like the fuel tanks they called *bidonnes*. There's a theory—one I heard from Ofer Gavish, a Phantom navigator in 1973 who later became a human repository for Israeli musical history—that the country's songs come from the same source as its weapons. So at the birth of the state, when the arms were mostly Czech and the inspiration communist, the tunes came from Russia. When the air force began flying Mirages and Mystères, the Israeli singers and artists who mattered were all visiting Paris and bringing back Piaf and Moustaki and translated *chansons*. Then came the late sixties, when the French chose the Arabs over the Jews, and the weapons started coming from America with rock 'n' roll.

Far beneath the pilots, the Golan escarpment was covered with the black spots of Syrian tanks moving into Israeli territory with little to stop them. The war on the ground was a different world from the one in the air, but black smoke rising from the battlefield reached the rarified height where the pilots worked, turning the whole scene dark.

Down below, the scale of what had gone wrong was clear from the first hours of the fighting. Entire units had vanished. In the air, however, the pilots' hubris was chipped but not shattered. The superheroes in the green flight suits were supposed to win this time as they'd won six years before. But this was a new war, and the enemy had new missiles from their Russian patrons, the same ones that Tom Wolfe described when he wrote about the air war over North Vietnam a few years earlier. The SAMs were like "flying telephone poles," he wrote, climbing toward you in clusters of six or eight, turning to follow you when you tried to get away: "The SAM's come up, and the boys go down."

The flight this morning, the second day of the war, was a choreographed plan known as Model 5. The idea was to destroy the Syrian missile batteries on the Golan so the

Israeli jets would be free to help the infantry and tank men who were screaming for air support down on the plateau. Some of the planes were flying from the Ramat David air base in northern Israel, a seven-minute flight to the war on the Golan if your plane was bomb-heavy and slow. Ofer, the Phantom navigator who later became a music historian, was at the base but was too green to fly a real mission at first. He was twenty-one and had been out of flight school for only a few months. He was preparing maps for the pilots and hanging around the operations room, listening to the radios.

The day before, he'd been home at his kibbutz for Yom Kippur. In those days many of the kibbutz movement's avowed atheists marked the fast day not just with a barbecue but with a *pork* barbecue, a way of celebrating their freedom from God and Jewish fate. That practice was about to change, one of many things that would change when the war made clear that no one was free of anything. When the call came from the squadron and Ofer rushed back to the base, one of the first things he saw was a veteran navigator, a religious Jew with a skullcap, asking the squadron's cook for a big steak. The navigator had flown one of the first desperate missions of the war while still fasting and almost fainted in the air. The religious Jew asking for a steak on Yom Kippur was one of Ofer's first indications of how bad things were. The navigator with the skullcap didn't survive the week.

The planes of Model 5 were sent off the following day at eleven a.m. to turn things around on the Syrian front. Ofer was reduced to hearing it from the base. At first there was radio silence. It was hard to imagine what was going on in the air. Some of his friends from the fresh batch out of flight school were raring to go, lobbying commanders to get on the roster, but Ofer was relieved to be on the ground. He wasn't eager to die in an airplane, or at all. If you meet him today it's impossible to believe he was anywhere near fighter jets. He's an elfin grandfather who leads tour groups around Israel with an acoustic guitar.

Before long, a flight of Phantoms from his squadron went in, led by a pilot named Henkin—they flew low to avoid enemy radar, pulled up into a steep climb, turned downward, and dove toward the batteries. It was all calculated to the foot, to the second, to the degree of the climb and the dive, based on aerial photographs that showed precisely where the batteries were. But the Syrians weren't stupid, and overnight they'd moved. Henkin was a pilot with a great future ahead of him, so they said. In the seat behind him was a navigator named Levi. They were already in the dive, the engine whining and the airplane shaking, when Henkin understood that his target wasn't there. He adjusted, but now the angle of the dive was steeper than planned—too steep, at least that's how the other pilots understood what happened. No one really knows.

Ofer was in the operations room when the squadron commander asked his pilots to report results. Someone said, "Number 1 went in next to the targets."

The commander said, "I understand that Number 1 went in to attack close to the targets?"

"No," said the voice. "He went into the ground next to the targets." The commander didn't want to understand what he was hearing.

What the pilots seem to remember more than anything else is the transitions. You were in the crew lounge, a kind of male paradise with armchairs, whisky, a record player, and women soldiers who worshipped and pitied you. There were cooks—reservists who'd been called up from hotels and cruise ships to make you food—and professional masseurs working on the Ping-Pong tables. Then the command arrived and you ran out to the tarmac. You climbed the ladder into your cockpit, sweating into your helmet and suit. Within a few minutes it was skidding telephone poles in the air and white carpets of cannon shells, and your friends exploding or parachuting into Egyptian fields to be pitchforked by villagers and taken to be tortured. If you made it, thirty minutes after takeoff you were back on the Ping-Pong table, getting oiled up. Then it was all black humour, poker, and the country's best bands, who started showing up at the base as soon as the war began—a hip new act called Beehive; a three-woman band called Chocolate, Mint & Gum, which included Yardena Arazi, famous as the prettiest woman in Israel. Then you strapped yourself in and went out again. One of the pilots compared it to "heating and cooling a piece of metal three times a day."

In the photographs everyone's grinning, of course. They're young and unfazed, chest hair surging from unzipped flight suits, moustaches and sideburns on the older reservists, nicknames like Rhino and Wild Bull, looking less like clean-cut American air-force types than like the military wing of Creedence Clearwater Revival. The base at Ramat David was a strange little world under intense psychological pressure.

The whole show was run by an officer who everyone called Zorik, the base commander, a wiry colonel who could fly any plane and whose leadership style was more personable than intimidating.

One night that first week, a Skyhawk pilot named Momo was asleep at the base. He was from Ofer's class at flight school, so he was also too green for combat. One of the experienced pilots who'd been called back from civilian life was a guy named Diamant, who was twenty-five, studying in university, and working with his father in construction. He had a little son and daughter. Diamant was suiting up in his quarters when a Syrian missile hit nearby and killed him. Momo heard the blast and scrambled under his bed but crawled back out when he realized that the bed was unlikely to help. A few hours later Momo got his chance to fly.

Before dawn he was in the briefing room with two others, preparing for a bombing run to Port Said at the northern tip of the Suez Canal. The flight's Number 1 was Vilan, one of the squadron's most experienced men. Young Momo would be Number 3. He was surprised to find that Number 2 would be Col. Zorik himself, who'd barely slept since the beginning of the war but who knew his men were rattled and insisted on joining the day's first mission to raise morale.

Momo climbed the rungs of the Skyhawk's ladder and slipped in. The canopy closed. He followed the two older pilots in a straight line down the coast toward Egypt in the dark, hugging the ground to avoid the missiles, and at first light he was over Sinai, approaching a lagoon on the Mediterranean shore that had somehow turned pink. He flew closer. The flamingos were migrating, and thousands of them were resting on the water at dawn.

The three planes turned inland. The green pilot saw the roads in northern Sinai backed up with Israeli vehicles, some of them stuck in the sand. The pilots skimmed the lagoons toward Port Said and pulled up into the attack about two miles out, lining up in the air, first Vilan, then Col. Zorik, then Momo in the Number 3 plane, which was the worst job because the first two might catch the Egyptian gunners by surprise, but by the time he showed up they'd definitely be waiting.

Vilan's plane rocketed into the sky and released its bombs. The gunners were still asleep. Then came Col. Zorik, and now Momo saw lines of shells rising from Port Said and thousands of bullets coming at him from infantry in the sand—he couldn't see the men, just their tracers in the dim light. He was flying into a white cloud of shell smoke and there was nothing he could do but ignore it, concentrating on the pull-up spot, the angle and speed of his climb, the force pushing his body into the seat, the light jerk of the bomb release, and he was away. He saw the flashes of light weapons coming from the reef by a besieged Israeli outpost called Budapest. Every Egyptian foot soldier in the vicinity was shooting at him, but he doesn't remember being afraid, just angry: "I was furious that they were trying to kill me," he said. "Who were these sons of whores who dare try to kill me?" He dove with his machine gun, strafing them once, then flipping back and doing it again, finishing every round he had before he heard Number 1 on the radio, screaming, "Pull up! Pull up!"

Momo lifted his head and looked out to sea. He saw the plane piloted by Col. Zorik, on his morale-boosting mission, gliding toward the surface of the Mediterranean, skimming the water. It wasn't clear what was happening, and Zorik never said a word on the radio, he just disappeared into the sea in a white circle of froth and no one ever found him. When you played music at an air base, you played for people who had images like that fresh in their minds.

9

A SHIELD AGAINST THE ENEMY

Because the army seems to have kept no account of Cohen's tour in the war and Cohen himself didn't keep a detailed journal, it's hard to pin down precise dates for the concerts. We have undated photographs, and Cohen's point-form list, and the memories of people who remember seeing him "early" or "late" in the fighting. We know the concerts happened, but we rarely know exactly when. It's possible, however, to come up with a rough order. Because Oshik's contacts were in the air force, the improvised band started there, beginning far from the front at an airfield called Hatzor, a drive of just an hour or two from Tel Aviv.

Ofer and Momo, the green navigator and pilot who'd just lost their commander at the northern air base Ramat David, had a friend at this other base whose name was Moshe, but who everyone called by a girl's name, Shoshi. He flew a Super Mystère, an old French plane on its way out of service. It lacked radar, and the bombsight was just a simple cross projected on glass. A neighbouring Phantom squadron, the 201st, was the hardest hit of all the squadrons in the war, and the list of missing pilots at the base grew longer and longer. Shoshi had seen the SAMs exploding in the air. He'd already heard that two kids from his kibbutz had been killed in their tanks.

In one mission over Suez a friend of his named Hagai, an artist by inclination, was patrolling at twenty thousand feet, looking out for SAMs rising from the desert floor as Shoshi dive-bombed the Egyptians. It was a tactic the pilots had developed to compensate for the lack of warning systems in their old aircraft. Shoshi dove toward an Egyptian invasion bridge, released his bombs, and had pulled up and away when someone on the radio said, "Number 3 is hit." Three was Hagai. There was no parachute, no airplane debris, nothing. He was just gone.

A few minutes passed, maybe less, it's hard to remember. Shoshi struggled to grasp how someone he knew could just vanish in an instant. A disembodied voice came on the emergency frequency. It was Hagai, back from the dead, speaking on the portable radio attached to his flight suit. He was floating far above them with his parachute at twenty thousand feet—he was in the sky above the planes, above the desert and the canal, looking down at the whole war like God himself. It was a time of wonders.

Because the primitive French planes couldn't do much at night, when darkness fell the pilots killed time on the ground, which is what Shoshi was doing when someone came out of nowhere and said Leonard Cohen was in the base's movie theatre. It was like news of an alien landing. What was Leonard Cohen doing here?

Shoshi knew Cohen's songs because on his kibbutz in southern Israel he and his friends used to put them on speakers and sprawl on the grass—"Suzanne," "Bird on the Wire." He also played them to girls for romantic purposes. But they were transmissions from the great world, not from here. He walked over to the theatre with a friend and found it packed with a few hundred people from the base's air and ground crews. Cohen was really there. He was already singing.

This first concert is the one Oshik remembers best. He opened by performing his own hits, which all the soldiers knew from the radio. Then he ran through a few comic skits with Pupik—these, to judge from one Pupik recorded around this time, were mostly funny voices, ethnic accents, and army jokes. In the recording, Pupik plays a senior officer surprising an addled new recruit on guard duty. Recruit, with rifle: "They said keep watch—how should I know how to keep watch? I don't know how to use this thing, where's the clutch?" Pupik, sternly: "Are you the patrol?" Recruit: "No sir, I'm Moshe." After that, the young Matti Caspi got up and played his songs, staring out at the crowd with his cryptic half smile and glassy eyes under curly hair. Then Leonard Cohen came out. "The audience went crazy," Oshik said. "They didn't believe it."

Matti Caspi accompanied Cohen on the guitar, and there was tension between Cohen's deceptively simple chords and Caspi's more ornate style. When the Israeli started elaborating on Cohen's song, taking it off in some direction of his own, Oshik remembered, Cohen mugged a surprised face and the crowd cracked up. When the show was over, an air force cultural officer came over and begged them to play again for the soldiers who hadn't been able to get in.

In the break before the second show, the Hatzor air base entered music history. It was then, on the first day of the war tour, that Cohen wrote a song. This is borne out by the notebook that Cohen had with him, an orange one with a doodle of three old-fashioned keys on the back cover. Inside are scribbles, half thoughts, and a few drafts of songs and poems. The first page reads:

HYDRA OCTOBER 1973

How lovely to be totally bankrupt

Then, on the next page:

TEL AVIV

who is what is speaking
from the fur on the floor of the sea

And then a full poem that starts (and your breath catches, if you know Cohen's work, because you're watching the birth of something famous):

I asked my father I asked
him for another name
I said the one I've got is soiled with fear and shame

It's an early version of "Lover Lover Lover," from the album Cohen would release after the war. He'd still be playing it in concerts decades later.

The subject of this first verse is interesting, considering the audience, the artist, and the time. Many of the Israelis in the room had exchanged Jewish names associated with the helplessness of the Diaspora for new Hebrew ones. Matti Caspi's father, for example, chose that Hebrew family name to replace Argentero, the name he'd brought with him from Serbia. Momo, the Skyhawk pilot, whose first name was really Shlomo, changed his family name from Zaltzman to Liran. The prime minister, Golda Meir, was previously Golda Meyerson. A lot of Jews, not just Israelis, were trying escape names like "Leonard Cohen." Issur Danielovitch became Kirk Douglas. Robert Zimmerman became Bob Dylan.

Cohen introduced "Lover Lover Lover" in the second show at the air base, according to both Oshik, who was standing by the stage listening, and Matti Caspi, who played guitar on the very first performance of the song. Caspi remembers Cohen still working on the song during the show and fine-tuning it as the band progressed through the war. Part of the evolution is visible in the notebook, where not all the verses are similar to the final version. The most striking difference involves a verse that stood out to the Israeli audience more than the others and which later vanished entirely. But some of the verses in the first draft, like this one, are close to the version we know:

He said I gave you this body for a trial
you can use it as a
weapon or to make
a woman smile

If these lyrics are a conversation with a specific audience—Israeli pilots and soldiers engaged in bloodshed—you might sense judgment in that line: God is testing humans, seeing which choice they'll make, war or love. The audience was engaged in the first, and Cohen the second. But of course the audience didn't really have a choice, as Cohen knew. It makes more sense that Cohen meant both uses were possible at different times. In any case, the singer wished them well as they flew out to face the SAMs, and in subsequent versions the song became a kind of talisman:

And may the spirit of this song
May it rise up pure and free
May it be a shield for you
A shield against the enemy

Did Cohen really think a song could protect these young people? He mentions the same idea in his manuscript about the war. "I said to myself, Perhaps I can protect some people with this song," he wrote. Perhaps he thought that if your spirit is fortified in battle at the crucial moment—by deep wisdom, a blessing, a love letter, a song—you'll know to dive, or swerve, or pull the trigger when necessary. There are ideas like that woven around the character of Arjuna, the warrior, in the Hindu tradition. But a simpler explanation for this verse is closer to Cohen's own upbringing. One of the duties of a priest, a Cohen, in Judaism is to stand in front of the congregation and call down divine protection: "May God bless and guard you." Invoking this shield is what a Cohen does.

Absent in the notebook draft is the chorus, "Lover lover lover lover lover lover lover come back to me." In fact, it's not immediately clear what links that chorus and the verses. Maybe the word *lover* appears here in the sense of the Song of Songs, where God's presence is described in terms of erotic love. Few require this presence as urgently as soldiers. Or maybe it's just a classic war chorus, an expression of longing for someone far away, like Konstantin Simonov's "Wait for Me," the favourite poem of the Red Army *frontoviki* of World War II. Each verse starts, "Wait for me and I'll come back." Cohen's mother, Masha, was a native Russian speaker, and maybe she sang him one of the musical versions of the poem when he was a child in the years of the world war. That sentiment, longing, is the one most likely to strike a chord with soldiers, far more than patriotism, anger, or despair. Researchers studying the music of GIs in Vietnam found that although movies after the war made it seem like the in-country soundtrack was political, with songs like "For What It's Worth" and "Fortunate Son," the songs the troops actually loved were the ones about loneliness and yearning, like "Leaving on a Jet Plane." Cohen's text worked on different frequencies, like the best prayers. The melody served the function ascribed to music by the Hasidic rabbis, that is, to make feeling and meaning available to those unable or unwilling to understand the words, or even to suggest feelings and meanings for which words fall short.

The young Mystère pilot Shoshi, who arrived late in his dirty flight suit amid the most frightening and exhilarating days of his life, doesn't remember "Lover Lover Lover," or anything else that Cohen played that night. He doesn't know if he was at the first show or the second. But he never forgot what it was like to be there.

When he squeezed into the theatre with his friend, the only place left was on the floor right in front of Cohen, between the front-row seats and the low stage. Cohen was in the middle of a song, so they sat down as quietly as they could. But the singer noticed. "He saw us, I saw that he saw us. We were close to him and maybe there was a bit of light," Shoshi said. "We were two kids in flight suits. I remember him looking at us a lot—at least that's what I remember. I don't know if that's what he'd remember. The war was at its height. We had losses. It spoke to me. The melodies were familiar. We didn't understand all the words, but it penetrated the heart."

At the second air base, Ramat David in the north, Shoshi's green friends from flight school remember a plane limping home from the front full of holes, and when it seemed about to touch down it blew up instead, scattering parts over the runway. There was a crippled Skyhawk that made it all the way back from the canal and came within sight of the runway before the pilot gave up and ejected, firing himself up into the air as the huge machine crashed into a shower and killed a few men from one of the ground crews. The pilots at the southern base, Hatzor, bragged over the telephone that they'd just seen Leonard Cohen. The pilots at the northern base were proud of the Israeli acts that had showed up to play for them—the Beehive, the Pale Tracker Trio, the local A-list—but Leonard Cohen was a celebrity of a different order. They were jealous. More missions went by, and more deaths, before Ofer, the Phantom navigator, heard someone shouting at him to run across the base to the lawn outside the 110th Skyhawk squadron. Cohen was here.

When Ofer arrived, someone else was playing. It wasn't Cohen. Maybe there had been a mistake. He pushed his way through the crowd and stopped close to the front, next to a man in a black sweater. After a moment he realized the man was Leonard Cohen, waiting his turn to sing.

There was no stage, just mikes set up on the grass and a small amplifier that had seen better days. Matti Caspi stood next to Cohen in light slacks and a plaid shirt.

"He announced 'Lover Lover Lover,' and said it was a new song," Ofer remembered. "We were surprised that he'd play a new song, we thought he'd only play the familiar ones, but he said, 'I want to play you something new.'" Someone standing behind Matti Caspi snapped a picture of the audience.

Ofer's friend Amos, a Skyhawk pilot, never forgot the mood of the show. "The experience, as I remember it, was forgetting everything and going to another world, one that wasn't all of us racing around, and the dead people, and the fear," he said. "I recall it as a formative event—one of the world's greatest singers coming in the middle of the war, amid all the chaos, bringing us some quiet and the sound of something else."

In the photograph, Amos can be seen in a striped shirt, sitting on the far left. Ofer is in the centre in a light-coloured shirt, arms draped over his knees. Behind him and to the left, looking intently at the performers with a half smile, is Momo, who on his first mission saw the base commander fly into the waves and disappear.

10

BROTHERS

After the missing verse of "Lover Lover Lover" in Cohen's orange notebook, eight lines appear under the title "Air Base." They were never published.

AIR BASE

I went down to the desert
to help my brothers fight
I knew that they weren't wrong
I knew that they weren't right
but bones must stand up straight and walk
and blood must move around
and men go making ugly lines
across the holy ground

This is the lost verse of "Lover Lover Lover." Soldiers heard Cohen sing it, and it appeared in an article written during the war by an Israeli reporter who was so moved by the message that he quoted this verse and none of the others. But the notebook draft shows Cohen beginning to distance himself almost immediately: in the second line, he crossed out the words "my brothers" and instead wrote, "the children." Then he discarded the verse altogether, and it surfaced only when I found it in the notebook. The lines might have been an authentic expression of a feeling Cohen had in the moment, but not of the way he felt when the war was over and he was back in the world. Or it's possible that the lines fit Leonard Cohen the private man, but not the artist.

Cohen always wrestled with the idea of commitment, but these thoughts seemed particularly intense around the time of the Yom Kippur War. He was nearly forty and a father. He'd just been on a long, strange trip through the sixties, a decade that cast off old strictures and identifications, but at thirty-nine you sometimes find yourself wondering if there's actually something to strictures and identifications. What if the answer wasn't in the Village or on a Greek island, but at the Gate of Heaven after all? Was marriage an archaic prison—or was it in fact "the hottest furnace of the spirit today," as Cohen once said, the only situation in which "any kind of work can be done"? What if the Jewish solution wasn't embracing the universal after all, but living in a small tribal state and speaking a language that no one else knew? What if these strange soldiers he'd never met were somehow his brothers? We know that Cohen was suspicious of people who made that kind of claim on him. "And if you call me

Brother now," he wrote in "Story of Isaac" a few years before, "forgive me if I enquire: Just according to whose plan?"

The Israeli musicians who travelled with Cohen say he asked them to use his Hebrew name, Eliezer. "Leonard" is hard for Israelis to pronounce: *leh-oh-narrrd*. Eliezer Cohen is a name so ordinary it's almost generic, and there were lots of them in the army. There was a famously reckless helicopter pilot named Eliezer Cohen who now commanded an air base in Sinai, and a Pvt. Eliezer Cohen who was killed at nineteen by a mine near the Gulf of Suez four years earlier, and another Pvt. Eliezer Cohen who was killed by a mine two years before that. The first Israeli across the Suez Canal when the counter-attack came in 1973 was a Lt. Eli Cohen. "Leonard" was a foreigner. "Eliezer" was a sibling.

Cohen felt the pull of this group of people. He wouldn't surrender to it completely, but it was why he came. Most artists who identified with the left weren't going to play in wars, because it might seem they approved. You needed to be sophisticated enough to see through the politics to the humanity of the soldiers, which wasn't easy in those years, when people called the veterans coming back from Vietnam "baby-killers." Johnny Cash and his wife, June Carter, went to Vietnam in 1969 and spent a few weeks at an air base called Long Binh, singing for soldiers heading into the bush and for the ones coming back on the medevac helicopters. "I almost couldn't stand it," Cash wrote. And in 1968 James Brown went out with a few bandmates, despite the unpopularity of the war and despite the racial hatred that threatened Brown and America itself; the tour began just after the murder of

Martin Luther King, Jr. Brown first played the airfield at Tan Son Nhut, near Saigon, and then toured for sixteen days, performing two shows at every stop, rehydrating between gigs with an IV drip. "We didn't do like Bob Hope," Brown told an interviewer. "We went back there where the lizards wore guns! We went back there where the 'Apocalypse Now' stuff was going on." Lots of people didn't like the war. "Well, I don't like the war, either," he said, "but we have soul brothers over there."

In his manuscript, Cohen presents what he says is a letter from Asher, the American he met on the plane to Tel Aviv with his Israeli wife. In Cohen's description, Asher comes across like a hippy rabbi, a type of Jew that you met in the seventies—acolytes of the singing rabbi Shlomo Carlebach, people who'd come to the Torah via the Bhagavad Gita or acid. If Cohen's manuscript presents the character of Anthony, the British painter who tried to talk Cohen out of going to Israel, as the universalist voice of the bohemians on Hydra, then Asher and his wife, Margolit, are the counterweight. They represent commitment to Judaism, Israel, and marriage. Those three entanglements seem to have been linked in Cohen's mind, which is why at one point in his manuscript he swears a vow of chastity as he heads to Israel, "unless she is my True Wife."

The letter from Asher, which reached Cohen on Hydra after the war, is the continuation of a conversation they had in Israel. There was something in Cohen, Asher wrote, "that is beginning to cry out to be real and realized." Asher meant the poet's priestly lineage. Cohen's ancestral calling, he wrote, was buried under the false image of a despairing artist in bondage to the seductions of the world. "We know you are a Cohen—and that God's purposes are working fantastically here for the purification of the Sons of Levi—so what," Asher wanted to know, "are you doing out there?"

Cohen should get married, Asher thought. Jewish law governing the priests in the ancient Jerusalem Temple decreed that each had to offer a sacrifice on behalf of himself "and his house," which meant not a physical house but a wife. Asher too had been faced with a choice between the physical and the spiritual. "The battle in me was and is waging over which voice to listen to—but I have chosen Him who has chosen me, and there is no other choice—for all flesh is as grass."

It was time for Cohen to come back to the tribe and accept his role. "We believe that if you will receive the cape of the prophet Elijah, the Spirit of God will be on you to make you a real Cohen. But you have to be as determined to receive God's blessing as Elijah," he wrote.

> We urge you to return in His time to physical Jerusalem and the spiritual Jerusalem to be built in us together as He reigns in His holy city—us.
>
> Come back to me lover, lover, come back to me lover, lover*—
>
> With a real sense of missing a close brother who is like the wind,
>
> Love, Asher

The asterisk is in the original and leads to an explanation from Cohen at the bottom of the page: "This is a paraphrase of a line from a song that I said to him when we met on the beach at Herzlia for the for the second time."

Unlike some of the other acts that were playing for troops, Cohen wasn't going to make do with concerts at bases a safe distance from the fighting. He was going where the lizards wore guns. After the "Air Base" poem in Cohen's orange notebook, in capital letters, he copies out an old aviation saying, the kind of thing you might overhear at an air base:

THE ONLY REPLACEMENT FOR THE DC3
IS ANOTHER DC3

The DC-3 Dakota was a transport plane flying troops and gear to the front in Sinai. The manuscript describes what happened next: "We flew in a Dakota to the desert."

11

IN THE DESERT

Sinai after a week of war was field hospitals, sandy airstrips, tents flapping in the blast of rotors. The closer you got to the canal the more burned vehicles you saw, the soldiers' vacant stares more pronounced. The Israeli public still hadn't been informed of the scope of the army's failure, but down here it was clear. This was around the time that the outpost called the Pier, which had been holding out somehow along the canal since the surprise attack, finally surrendered to the Egyptians. I know someone who was there, went off to a prison camp with the other survivors, and came back whole in body only.

Some of the soldiers in Sinai remember the little groups of musicians who could be seen moving around the front—bell-bottomed figures silhouetted in the dust clouds, gripping guitars in the back of speeding army trucks, hitching helicopter rides. One navigator on a Hercules transport remembered a scene from the Refidim air base, a snapshot that came to him as we spoke: He's just landed to ferry out casualties. A surgeon he's met before, Dr. Haruzi, comes out of the operating theatre with his white coat covered in blood, waving his hands with a grim expression. He's lost a patient. Nearby a few artists—long hair, civilian clothes, one with a guitar—wait for someone to get them out of here.

After landing near the front, Cohen and the band were issued sleeping bags. They had a small amp which they'd have to hook up to the batteries of tanks or trucks. They set off, sometimes as a group and sometimes alone. Nowhere in his pocket notebooks or typed manuscript does Cohen give any indication that he knows where he is. Other than Jerusalem and Tel Aviv, there are no place names at all. Part of this was being a foreigner, but the experience of his Israeli companions doesn't seem to have been much different. They weren't combat soldiers. They were far from their cafés. Once they were at the front, it was all "the desert."

There was no organized tour. "Any idiot can come and take you," Oshik said, explaining how it worked. The "idiots" were the young Education Corps officers whose job it was to bring singers to units in the field. "We have no idea where we are, and no idea who these guys are. Every day a different education officer comes, or some other idiot, and says, 'Eight of our guys just got killed, you have to come.' Hey, where are we going? Why? But what can I say to them? They put you in the truck and you go."

I spent a long time trying to track down a record of dates and locations, or someone who'd coordinated the concerts, but when I said the word *coordinated*, Oshik cracked up.

"These kids would come and argue with each other about who'd get us," he said. "Who had more fatalities, more woes."

And who would decide?

"They'd argue."

And you'd go with the winner?

"You can't say no to them. Can you say no?"

The audience wasn't always interested. It was one thing to round up bored soldiers in the rear, mechanics and cooks, but many combat troops weren't in the mood for civilians with guitars, smelling of girls and Tel Aviv, or for "education officers" who weren't dying. They preferred not to be reminded of a normal life from which they were locked out and which they might not see again. "Raising morale" is a civilian idea. The soldiers had seen something true and awful about the world, and they weren't going to be cheered up.

Sometimes soldiers were forced to listen or were too worn down to object. There's documentary footage of an entertainment troupe in 1973 where a few teenage musicians are frantically clapping and singing for an audience of filthy soldiers sitting on the ground, staring into space with hollow eyes. If you research the Yom Kippur War you'll see a lot of corpses, but this image is worse. It's one of the most awful of the war.

They moved deeper into the netherworld of the front. If they were playing during the day, Pupik, the comic, made sure the soldiers sat on a slope with the sun behind them— better for the performers to have the sun in their eyes than the audience. When they played in a bunker with a lightbulb dangling from the ceiling, he rigged an egg carton on one side of the bulb so the stage would be lit and the audience in the dark. Pupik also brought along a suitcase, not just to keep his clothes in, but as a prop: He'd step up to the microphone, then seem to notice that he was too short to reach it. He'd rush off stage, bring out his suitcase, and hop up. That usually got a laugh.

A typical concert, in Oshik's memory: An officer takes them out in the desert at night in a truck. The front is close but he doesn't know how close. They stop by a few big artillery guns clustered in the sand. Everything is completely black. Does anyone want to hear some music? Some dirty soldiers gather around. Pupik builds a stage of ammunition crates and arranges the truck's headlights for illumination. They start singing. Suddenly an artillery officer says politely, "Can you stop for a moment," and shouts: "GUN THREE!" The ground shakes and the air ripples with the force of the projectile. Everyone is deafened for a few seconds. They begin singing again.

12

TEA AND ORANGES

Not everyone at the front knew who Cohen was, but if they did, the song they knew was "Suzanne." He seems to have played it at most or all of the shows, and in his recollections, Cohen recounts travelling in the desert: "I'm killing an arrogant Israeli officer who won't stop bugging me to sing 'Suzanne.' The balance is returned. Justice is done. It's not certain I'm making that up."

Today Cohen might be the foreign artist whose songs are translated and performed most often in Israel. New Hebrew versions of Cohen songs appear every year, and some songs, like "Lover Lover Lover," have been translated more than once. By the time Cohen showed up in the war, there was already a version of "Suzanne" circulating in Hebrew. It was the work of a singer-songwriter named Gidi Koren, founder of a band called the Brothers and Sisters, a name he chose as a tribute to the Mamas and the Papas. Gidi loved "Suzanne." It was so different from everything else he'd heard, so strange to Israeli ears. His translation, which might have been the first Hebrew version of a Cohen song, was performed but never recorded and was eventually forgotten, surviving only as a file on Gidi's computer.

The Brothers and Sisters were a popular band but you couldn't make a living from music in Israel in those days, and that wasn't Gidi's real job. He'd just finished medical school and was an intern at a hospital near Tel Aviv. He was twenty-six, with a small daughter and a pregnant wife. He was in the middle of a shift on Yom Kippur when the army suddenly started pulling staffers from the ward, when "the music started," as he put it, meaning the sound and rhythm of an Israeli crisis.

Helicopters began thumping outside and soon the orderlies were rushing into the burn unit with figures in torn green uniforms, men his age coming in scorched all over from explosives, mostly third-degree, the kind of burn that penetrates the skin and muscle and brings your chances far down. They were coming from their tanks along the Suez Canal via overwhelmed field hospitals in Sinai. He did what he could— liquids, morphine, disinfection. Some of them could be saved, and later they'd get new skin, but a lot of them were lost by the time they arrived. The senior hematologist would come around and Gidi watched her stand by the beds and decide when to turn off the machines.

When the war got worse, Gidi was sent down to help in the field, taking a transport flight to one of the big air bases in Sinai and then overland to a hospital—a few tents and shipping containers, a mobile operating room, hot blasts of sand as the choppers landed with more green figures on stretchers. He doesn't remember where it was, just "the desert." The mood was as dark as you'd expect, not just because of the work but because the wounded soldiers were bringing in the worst news of the war—battles gone wrong, whole units up in smoke. He doesn't remember individual stories. He didn't want to see these figures as people with names. By this time he already had news of the kids he'd grown up with: Lipa Milnov had been killed, and Menachem Silman, and Yakov Sofer from the soccer team. More soldiers came in, unconscious from blood loss or morphine. He applied bandages like a robot and moved the figures from tent to tent, and someone said Leonard Cohen was outside.

That didn't make any sense. But Gidi went out into the sunlight and there he was, just Cohen, in fatigues like any other soldier. Gidi didn't dare speak to Cohen or say anything about translating "Suzanne." He can't remember why. He doesn't think Cohen was inaccessible. The presence of Leonard Cohen at this field hospital was so unlikely that he may not have believed it was actually happening, like all of the other things that he was seeing and doing.

Cohen was standing a few steps away from him, playing his guitar. The medics and doctors and nurses stood opposite the singer in bloody smocks. For a moment, no helicopters landed. The scalpels rested on trays and the tents were quiet. Cohen sang "Suzanne."

13

NO WORDS

"We drove hundreds of kilometres in a Volkswagen van, double-cabin, with combat rations," Pupik recalled. "Desert without end."

On one road near the canal, Pupik sat in the back of a truck, bumping around in the dust and noise. He doesn't think Cohen was with him this time. A plume rose ahead of the truck, "as if someone kicked the sand with his foot." Then another one. They were being shelled, so they turned the truck around and raced back, stopping at an intersection where they all got out to pee from relief until a few soldiers pulled up in a jeep and screamed at them that the Egyptians were zeroed in on all the intersections, so they jumped back into the truck and sped further back behind Israeli lines. You had to be careful, but even if you were, it wouldn't necessarily help. There was one rising star, the singer Roman Sharon, twenty-three years old and handsome, who was leaving a show at the Refidim air base when an army semi-trailer hit his truck and killed him.

Cohen requested no special treatment. When the performers reached a base they'd just throw sleeping bags on the floor of the PX or some other room, but they thought Cohen might have different standards and offered to find him a real bed. He said no. He slept on the floor and ate combat rations like everyone else. That meant something to the Israelis. "I was so impressed by him that I treated him with awe. We didn't talk like friends," Pupik remembered. "I tried to open a door to get to him, but he didn't open up, maybe just a crack. But he was someone who gave off an aura of good-heartedness, of unusual humanity."

Pupik was a member of the Tel Aviv bohemian set centred on the charismatic degenerate Uri Zohar, an actor, and the singer Arik Einstein. The kibbutz socialists of the founding generation had discarded Jewish tradition, and young people like Pupik weren't interested in socialism or the kibbutz, or in ideology of any kind, so what was left was just sunshine and the beach and whatever urge struck you. After the Yom Kippur War some of them realized this wasn't enough, they needed a reason for things, and fled the emptiness back to old-time religion. It was partly the shock of the war, and partly the post-sixties hangover that began to be felt across the Western world, and partly because they were getting older. Eventually even the ringleader, Uri Zohar himself, disappeared into the world of black hats in Jerusalem and remains there to this day. But Pupik was one of the first to go. He gave up on secular life right after the war, hanging up his flamboyant striped bell-bottoms. When I met him in his small apartment in Jerusalem, he was known as Rabbi Mordechai

Arnon. He had a big black skullcap and a long grey beard through which it was barely possible to see the face of the sprite from the old photos.

Cohen was interested in Judaism, he remembered, and knew a lot about it. Pupik didn't. He knew so little about his own civilization that he "wasn't a Jew." He knew songs and parties, the life of the new Israelis freed of the hang-ups and nightmares of their parents. And he knew hashish, which everyone smoked, but which he says he smoked more than everyone.

On Yom Kippur, Pupik was back home with his parents at their scrappy agricultural collective. Pupik saw significance in the following story, which he told me carefully. You can hear the hoarse laugh of history somewhere in here, just out of reach. Leonard Cohen would get it.

Pupik still had no interest in religion but thought the fast would be a good way to kick his smoking habit, because that was also forbidden on the Day of Atonement. He was unhappy with his life and wanted to regain control. So he was in syn-agogue for the first time in years, and after the prayer of Unetaneh Tokef and the famous list of the many ways to die, after the end of the midday service and before the Book of Jonah, he was out on the street and a man came up to him.

The man was in his fifties. He asked in Yiddish for a cig-arette. The comic had come here to stop smoking, and the man was looking for a cigarette on Yom Kippur! But Pupik wanted to help, so he took the man over to his childhood home, where his parents were resting before the afternoon service, and gave him a pack of cigarettes. The man ducked his head behind the balcony wall so he couldn't be seen from the street, lit up, and inhaled. He said, still speaking Yiddish: I'll tell you why I smoke on Yom Kippur.

We were eighteen, the man said, when the world war broke out. We were drafted to fight in the Red Army. What's the first thing you take? *Mahorka*, bags of tobacco to roll. So we're riding in the troop train, singing songs to keep the spirit up, and I'm smoking a cigarette, when one of the other Jewish soldiers, a righteous Jew, suddenly bangs on the wall and shouts in Yiddish, *raboisai!* Gentlemen! Today is Yom Kippur! It was the holiest day of the year, a fast day, and here he was on his way to a war, spitting in God's face by smoking.

Since then, the man said, exhaling, I can't let Yom Kippur go by without smoking a cigarette. He wandered off, and Pupik never saw him again. An hour later came the siren and the war started.

Later, when the comic found faith, he came to see divine intervention in the war's outbreak on Yom Kippur of all days. It's the only day of the year when Israel's roads are completely empty, which allowed the army to deploy quickly. That was the first miracle of the war, the first of many. "God is watching us to an extent that's unbelievable," said Rabbi Mordechai Arnon when we spoke forty-five years later. "All you need to do is open your eyes."

Back then he couldn't talk to Cohen about Judaism, but he did know something about astrology, so they talked about that. The Israelis spoke among themselves about music or philosophy, or sometimes just amused themselves with rambling, associative nonsense in keeping with the surreal life of those weeks. Cohen would sometimes sit out in the desert and look up at the stars. We don't know what the singer thought about his conversations with Pupik or the other Israelis, because he doesn't mention them in his writing. In fact, he doesn't mention the musicians who travelled with him at all. In Cohen's account he was there alone.

This might have something to do with Matti Caspi's response when I asked him about the tour. Of the four Israelis in the improvised band, Caspi was the most talented and the most successful later on. He's an icon here, like Cohen. It was Caspi who accompanied Cohen in the shows, and there's one photograph from the desert in which you see Cohen, uniquely, not playing but listening closely to someone else, and it's Caspi. I had found some of Caspi's written recollections but hoped he'd say more. He wouldn't. "I don't have anything to add about Leonard Cohen," he replied, "because no close connection was formed between us, and I don't like filling holes in the air."

The Israeli performers with Cohen were an interesting crew in their own right, and a few notable songs came out of their time together. Oshik, the balladeer, was carrying around a collection by the Hebrew poet Leah Goldberg, and somewhere on the road in Sinai he gave the book to Caspi, who selected "For Some Time," a poem that isn't about war at all, but about a woman's loneliness. Caspi wrote music, Oshik recorded it after the war, and the song is still famous. Caspi also managed to write a song about how the only honest response to a war is to say nothing. "We Have No Words" has an ironic, catchy tune so an audience can clap their hands and sing along:

> We have no words
> And we have no tune
> That's okay, we can always just sing "la la la"

There's footage of the four Israeli members of the band performing "We Have No Words" for soldiers after the cease-fire. It's the closest thing we have to footage of the tour itself. By this time Cohen's gone, but Matti Caspi is there with his odd, impersonal gaze; Rovina with her sculpted blond helmet and theatrical stance; Oshik with his shaggy hairdo and white turtleneck; and Pupik, cracking jokes from the side.

At the time, Pupik saw himself as a kind of comic warrior, sallying forth four or five times a day, indoors, outdoors, day and night, for people at the worst moment of their lives, some desperate for distraction, others wishing they were anywhere but at the show. When he improvised skits, he was like a trapeze artist. The crowd below wasn't just wondering if he'd fall, but hoping he would. "Every show is a battle," he said. "You have to defeat the audience." Cohen's onstage persona at this time couldn't have been more different than that of the antic comedian, but he had a similar idea about performing. A year after the war he was asked by a Spanish journalist about his "severe attitude onstage," his resistance to cracking a smile. "There are those who sing laughing, who prance around and make a show," Cohen said. "I sing serious songs, and I'm serious onstage because I couldn't do it any other way. I think that a bullfighter doesn't enter the ring laughing. Rather, he enters thinking that he is betting his life against the bull."

They were driving through the desert in the Volkswagen, Pupik told me, down miles of empty highway, when they stopped near an improvised structure with poles and a burlap roof. They sat in the shade to eat and were immediately beset by flies. They weren't sure why, until someone said, "Hey, look at that." Sticking out of a little pile of sand was a boot. It was attached to a leg. They were surrounded by corpses half-covered in sand.

14. We sang wherever men were gathered, sometimes in halls for hundreds, or beside anti-aircraft guns for tens or twenties. Sometimes there were lights, other times they would shine flashlights at us. We sang wherever we were asked.

15. Calluses developed on my fingertips. There were suggestions here and there that I was useful.

16. The only Replacement for a DC3 is another DC3.

17. Men were getting killed. I began to end our show with a new song. The chorus was: Lover lover lover lover lover lover lover come back to me.

18. I said to myself, Perhaps I can protect some people with this song. I would keep it going for a long time.

14

ALREADY WET

As Cohen and his comrades progressed into the combat zone, other musicians were travelling from unit to unit in the desert and along the northern front on the Golan Heights. The army's disarray was such that no one seemed to really know where the artists were, or they made sure they stayed a safe distance from the fighting.

The singer Avner Gadasi remembered being sent north from Tel Aviv with another performer and arriving on the Golan Heights. They drove up to a base that had just been lost to the Syrians, then recaptured. Almost no one was alive. "The guard at the gate told us, 'Go straight uphill and see if there's anyone left to play for,'" he told a journalist. "We went in. You see fire, burning barrels, burnt papers, you see that this place has been through a terrible ordeal. They'd burned things to keep them out of enemy hands. Amid all of this we found a few soldiers, maybe ten. They brought a bulldozer and we sat on its shovel, like a little stage, and we played for them."

The singer Yardena Arazi volunteered as soon as the war started. There's a photo of her singing at an air base with her trio Chocolate, Mint & Gum, three young women in jeans and T-shirts, Arazi with her famous black braids. She reached the Golan escarpment along with the reinforcements racing to shore up the faltering troops in the Israeli line. Like many entertainers, including Pupik, she'd started out in the most famous military entertainment troupe, the one attached to a brigade called the Fighting Pioneer Youth. She learned the trade during the attrition battles in the late 1960s along the Suez Canal, where the troupe would travel from out-post to outpost, and where one of her musician friends had his leg nearly severed by shrapnel. But this was the first time she saw dead Israelis. "I remember one concert on the Golan for paratroopers who'd lost a lot of friends. They weren't in the mood," she told a reporter years later. It was dark. The musicians used jeep headlights for illumination. They sang a classic from the '48 war called "Friendship," about fallen comrades, a song beloved of the parents of these soldiers. When the song was written, at the moment of Israel's birth, the Jews thought it would be just one war and that's it. But there had been three since then. It was like the war was never going to end. "They cried, and we cried," she said.

These were performers the soldiers knew as part of their own story. Cohen wasn't one of them. He sang in a different language about people and places far away. But soldiers in a war don't necessarily want to hear songs about war or about where they are. They want to be somewhere else. Music that's too happy won't work either, because it's too distant and makes light of their lives.

I remember a tour in the security zone in south Lebanon in 1998, after which my infantry company went for a week of R&R and they brought a pop star to play for us. She had a hit just then called "Unload Your Weapon, My Soldier" which was all double-entendres and dance moves that she performed with two male dancers who had faux-military uniforms and little plastic guns. We stood and stared at them. It was awful. At the time I resented our officers for forcing us to be there, and resented her for thinking she could possibly have something to say to us. Now my emotion is mostly empathy for the poor singer. I wonder what she was thinking onstage, just as I wonder the same about Cohen, standing in the desert facing people facing death.

It seems reasonable to imagine that he wondered what these soldiers thought of him, and how he'd perform in their place if the roles were reversed. Perhaps he worried about a repeat of that Jerusalem concert, when something about the Israeli audience, even in much simpler circumstances, had cost him his nerve. He might have been asking, as he said he did when he froze at that show: "Where do you get to stand up and speak? For what and whom? And how deep is your experience? How significant is anything you have to say?"

He might have been thinking what any honest artist thinks all the time—Am I a fraud?

But here Cohen didn't freeze. As the days went by and he saw more and more soldiers, he must have felt that his art was working. His confidence can be gleaned from two short lines we've encountered in the manuscript, both of proletarian modesty. "Calluses developed on my fingertips," he wrote, which tells us that he hadn't touched a guitar for a long time and was now playing constantly. "There were suggestions here and there that I was useful."

It might have been the songs, or his presentation, or the fact that his outlook turned out to be precisely the one called for in these circumstances. "A pessimist is somebody who is waiting for the rain. Me, I'm already wet," he once said. "I don't wait for the rain to fall. We are in the catastrophe."

In an interview not long afterward, Cohen talked about distinct ways of dealing with disaster. "You have a tradition which says that if things are bad we should not dwell on the sadness," he said. "That we should play a happy tune, a merry tune." Then there's the Middle Eastern tradition, he explained, which "says that if things are really bad, the best thing to do is sit by the grave and wail. And that's the way you are going to feel better." Both approaches can help. "And my own tradition, which is the Hebraic tradition," he said, "suggests that you sit next to the disaster and lament. The notion of lamentation seemed, to me, to be the way to do it. You don't avoid the situation, you throw yourself into it."

If that's what he was doing, it came across even in a language that many of those listening didn't know. "When people think that a song has to make sense, Leonard would prove otherwise," Joan Baez once explained. "It doesn't necessarily make sense at all. It's just coming from so deep inside of him that it somehow or other touches deep inside of other people. I'm not sure how that works, but I know that it works." Baez was talking about Cohen's performance in 1970 at the chaotic rock festival on the Isle of Wight, where he had to play for a half million people who were wet, tired, and fed up, and who'd already heckled Baez, thrown bottles at Kris Kristofferson, and burned the stage with Jimi Hendrix on it. Looking bedraggled and defeated himself, Cohen appeared late at night. He strummed his guitar quietly and spoke to the crowd as if they were friends in a room. He had them light matches so he could see where they were. He hypnotized them. The whole masterful act was caught on film.

The Isle of Wight, however, wasn't the most relevant precedent for the way Cohen communicated with soldiers in Sinai. Neither was his previous brush with international conflict in 1961, when he travelled to Havana and happened to be there for the Bay of Pigs invasion. (A photograph survives of Cohen posing with two communist soldiers, wearing pseudo-revolutionary garb and looking silly.) The precedent was playing at mental asylums.

The first of these concerts was at Henderson Hospital near London in August 1970, two days before the Isle of Wight and three years before the war. Sylvie Simmons describes the show in her Cohen biography, *I'm Your Man*. The hospital had grim stone walls and a tower. A few of his bandmates from the Army were resistant but came around when Cohen insisted. Cohen didn't tell the band exactly why it was important to him, but they understood that he had empathy for people who'd gone over the edge and was familiar with the edge himself.

The shows were potent. There's a story that Ron Cornelius, the guitarist, told Simmons about a young man who stood up with a piece of his skull missing—you could see his brain beating through his skin—and started screaming at Cohen so loud that the band stopped playing. "The kid said, 'Okay, okay, big-time poet, big-time artist, you come in here, you've got the band with you, you've got the pretty girls with you, you're singing all these pretty words and everything, well what I want to know, buddy, is what do you think about me?'" Cohen walked off the stage and into the rows of seats, the guitarist remembered, "and before you knew it he had the guy in his arms, hugging him."

Cohen believed, as he told an interviewer, that the experience of mental patients "would especially qualify them to be a receptive audience for my work."

In a sense, when someone consents to go into a mental hospital or is committed, he has already acknowledged a tremendous defeat. To put it another way, he has already made a choice. And it was my feeling that the elements to this choice, and the elements of this defeat, correspond with certain elements that produced my songs, and that there would be an empathy between the people who had this experience and the experience as documented in my songs.

Soldiers aren't mental patients but sometimes they're not far, and some of them will be later on. In a war anyone who's honest knows they've been defeated, even if their side wins. Cohen had never seen a war, couldn't speak Hebrew, and couldn't make much sense of what was going on around him. He didn't know where he was. But he knew something about the audience.

"I was afraid at first that my quiet and melancholy songs weren't the kind that would encourage soldiers at the front," Cohen told a reporter from the Israeli paper *Yediot Ahronot* who caught up with him during the war, in one of the few quotes we have from Cohen in those weeks. "But I learned that these wonderful kids don't need glorious battle-anthems. Now, between battles, they're open to my songs maybe more than ever before. I came to raise their spirits, and they raised mine."

Cohen's tour didn't attract much public attention. There was too much else going on. There are just a few mentions in the Israeli papers, usually in articles about other stars who'd arrived from abroad and were more famous at the time, like Danny Kaye and the French singer Enrico Macias. (In the article quoted above, for example, Macias was in the headline and Cohen mentioned near the end.) A second quote survives from a radio report on the Voice of Israel, after a segment with Danny Kaye. "Another famous artist is the singer Leonard Cohen," the reporter says, "whose quiet protest songs challenge the idea of war. Modest, quiet, and looking younger than his age, he told me that only now that he's seen the war and its effects does he understand the difficulty, perhaps even the impossibility, of describing it in a poem or song. I asked him if his experiences here would be expressed in some way in his work."

Cohen's voice comes in with its careful Canadian cadence. "Oh, I really don't know," he says. "It's impossible for me to talk of it. I don't have anything to say. I'm just an entertainer here. Of course I have impressions of things I've seen. If they'll be expressed in my songs—I don't know yet. In any case, I didn't come here to collect material." There's a question from the interviewer that is unclear in the recording, and Cohen answers: "I don't have any thoughts about it. I just came as soon as I could."

15

PSYCHOLOGY

I know a psychologist named Joel who was a twenty-five-year-old medic at the time. He reached the war a week in, on October 13, when things were grim, before the counter-attack across the canal changed the picture two days later. On the day he arrived, General Albert Mendler, commander of all Israeli armoured forces in Sinai, was killed in his half-track.

When the siren went off during the Yom Kippur prayers, Joel was supposed to have been with a reserve unit at one of the Suez outposts, part of a routine call-up a few weeks before. But he'd been held up at the university, missed a bus, and by the time he reached the base the unit was gone. The army clerks sent him home. If he'd been on time, he would have been caught in the surprise attack and would now be dead or a prisoner. But instead he was at a synagogue in Jerusalem.

Even though it was Yom Kippur, when the use of electricity is forbidden, the rabbi said it was permissible to turn on the radio, because the call-up codes of different units were being read out on air. Driving to the induction centres was also permissible, because Judaism places the principle of saving human life above other religious strictures, even the laws of Yom Kippur.

In the bedlam of the induction centres Joel met someone he knew who was studying medicine in Italy. The army clerks assigned this medical student to an armoured battalion and Joel to the paratroops, even though, unlike the medical student, Joel had been in a tank unit and had never jumped out of a plane. It was army logic. The two of them tried to switch assignments, but the clerks had already made carbon copies of the lists. It was too much trouble to change them. The medical student was killed by a mine.

His company of paratroops got to Sinai a few days later and ended up somewhere south of the Mitleh Pass, he isn't sure where. They were in trucks in the desert when they heard that General Mendler was dead. That's how he dates his arrival in the war. Otherwise he'd have no idea.

They were carrying heavy gear over the dunes. He was out of shape and had trouble keeping up. He doesn't remember the order of things, just snapshots: Four Israeli tanks on a rise in front of him, facing the enemy, then four explosions, one after the other. The desert floor covered with fine filaments like a spider's web, you'd trip over them, you'd see them gleaming in the sun, they were beautiful—the guiding wires of Egyptian rockets. The Israeli tanks were a few hundred yards away. Joel reminded his lieutenant that he was a medic and asked if he should go over to help. Only if you have a spatula, the lieutenant said. Every once in a while you'd see a blackened figure in tank coveralls coming at you from the sand, asking where you're from, looking for somewhere to go. No one at home knew who was dead or alive or a prisoner. Joel's parents were in Boston and he knew they were worried, so he wrote them a letter on the back of a label he peeled off a can of army peas. The unit got a crate of new shoulder-launched rockets from an American shipment. A soldier standing near Joel fired one by mistake, and it just missed him. Joel's war story was about near misses.

The famous singer Yehoram Gaon came to perform for them. He was being driven all over the front, stopping for groups of soldiers, and by the time he reached Joel and his friends he had no voice left and couldn't sing. He apologized.

There was a barrage and someone shouted something that sounded like *esh ness!* Joel didn't understand what that meant. He'd come from America only a few years earlier, fresh from Boston University in 1969, with not much beyond a tape recorder and some Dylan, Rabbi Carlebach, and Leonard Cohen. His Hebrew still wasn't great, but he knew *esh* was fire and *ness* was a miracle, and thought maybe they were talking about a kind of miracle firebomb or something, but actually the word *ness* here meant something different, it was a Hebrew acronym for a massive anti-battery barrage. It meant this was the kind of barrage you should run away from. They all ran to the half-tracks to escape, but there was one guy named Bar-On who just stood there petrified in the barrage, not running anywhere. He wouldn't listen to reason and just stood there. Joel was looking back on this event as a psychologist in his seventies. They had to use "psychology" on this soldier, he remembered, which meant that one of the others ran up to him and punched him in the face, and then they threw him in the half-track.

He was up all night and finally, in the middle of the day, came to a place where they were allowed to rest for a few hours. It wasn't a base, just a temporary camp in the sand. He fell into a deep sleep with his boots on. He passed out as you do when you're a soldier—partly from exhaustion, partly because alcohol and drugs are unavailable and sleep is the only way to block out what's going on. No civilian slumber is as deep. He was asleep when he heard the voice. He knew who it was.

"I heard the singing and thought, well, obviously I'm dreaming," he remembered. "I tried to get up, but I couldn't. I fell back. I heard it again, and I said no—I have to get up and see what's going on." This happened three, maybe four times. But he couldn't wake up. In the end he fell into an even deeper sleep. "I thought, it can't be true, but it's a beautiful dream so I'm going to keep on dreaming."

After a while some other soldiers shook him awake and he came to in the sand. There was an ambush that night and they had to get ready. They said a singer had come, an American Jew with a guitar, no one they knew. He played a few songs and drove off. No, Joel said—it couldn't be. But it was. It really was Cohen in Sinai. He missed that too.

16

RESPITE

In the Book of Jonah there's a scene where the wayward prophet has finally discharged his divine mission in Nineveh. Now he's in open land outside the city, sitting in the fierce sun. He's been through a lot—a shipwreck, the belly of the fish. God summons up a plant which spreads with supernatural speed over Jonah's head, giving him shade and bringing him "great happiness." Maybe he's finally figured it all out. In fact, God is about to send a worm to kill the plant and continue Jonah's education, but the hero doesn't know it yet.

Cohen and the band were given a respite:

Dakota took us back to Lod. We were driven into Tel Aviv. I felt very strong. I didn't corner Aleece, I didn't hunt for Rochel. I drank with the War Correspondents at the bar in the Dan Hotel. I was a serious fellow who had seen the war.

17

THE STORY OF ISAAC

No one in Tokyo knew it was Yom Kippur. Isaac isn't sure he knew. He was as far as he could go from Israel and Jews and his kibbutz and Almond Reconnaissance, from hunting infiltrators on the Gaza border. He was done with the army and out in the world, past the outer limits, selling paintings on the underground—Ginza Line, Marunouchi Line, Toei Line 1. Kyobashi Station, Toranomon Station, Akasaka-mitsuke. White-gloved conductors. Neon reflections on wet asphalt. Schoolgirl braids and Elvis haircuts.

He had no plans to go home. But when the news came, Isaac knew his friends would be in the thick of it, and the need to be with them overruled everything else. He took his little Toyota to a garage and left it there with a note asking the mechanic to send him $600 to Israel, but never got the money. Then he took the little he had saved and tried to get a flight from Japan heading west.

Isaac had a friend from Almond Reconnaissance named Shlomi, who was on the other side of the world in London, working as an air marshal for El Al. In the Israeli army, the unit called Almond is a legend from the old days, when there were still wild units operating outside the rules. The soldiers from Almond had their own goat herd. They took turns on shepherd duty. They were mostly kids fresh from the fields of the kibbutzim, educated in practical communism and the ideals of secular humanism, and good at war. The unit didn't believe in taking prisoners. If you fought Almond Reconnaissance either they died, or you did. The spirit came from the Bedouin fighter Abd el-Majid Hidr, who'd decided to be someone else, changed his name, and became the Israeli commander Amos Yarkoni. He had one arm. It's a long story.

Isaac and Shlomi had served under an officer who was blond and a bit crazy, one of the best young field commanders in the army. No one used his real name, which was Amatzia. Everyone called him Patzi. There are lots of stories about Patzi. Once, a few years before the war, the Almond soldiers were on a raid deep in Jordan and fought their way back to the Israeli border, but just barely. They were about to cross to safety when Patzi stopped the whole force in enemy territory. He reminded everyone that it was Purim, the raucous festival of masks and inebriation, and forced them all to stand there and sing Purim songs to his satisfaction before he agreed to lead them home.

Some of the Almond stories sound like Irish ballads or country songs. There was one incursion into Jordan where the soldiers killed a mare by mistake. They laid an ambush for guerrillas and the horse surprised them. In the morning they discovered a beautiful red foal grazing near its mother's body, and being farm kids, they lassoed it, brought it grass, and took care of it in the house where they were holed up. When the unit returned to Israel, one of the lieutenants snuck the foal over the border in a half-track and took it to live on his kibbutz in the north. He left the army when he got his girlfriend pregnant, went for a stint of reserve duty along the Suez Canal, and was blown up by an Egyptian mine, leaving a baby daughter and the Jordanian foal. After that (so the story goes) the lieutenant's father never said much. He moved his bed into the stable and raised the red foal like a son. The horse's descendants still canter around northern Israel.

From Tokyo, Isaac managed to get a flight to Rome, where the El Al desk was mobbed and turning people away. But they were letting infantry officers through. That's how he made it all the way from Japan to his kibbutz, Evron, which is on the coast near the border with Lebanon. He'd been away for a long time and hadn't expected to be back. No one knew he was coming. He walked through the gate and up the road to the factory that made irrigation valves. That's where he was, with his shaggy traveller's beard and his backpack, when his father pedalled by on a bike, busy with his work, steering with his right hand and holding a wooden ladder with his left. His father didn't see him.

Isaac's father, Michael, was a small man who'd been an executive at a department store in Budapest. Michael had another family before Isaac was born, a wife and two daughters, who were two and four. All three were killed by the Germans, but Michael survived in a forced-labour unit whose members were sent to walk through minefields. If you lost a foot, the Germans just shot you. He ended up living to 102.

Isaac's mother was married to another husband before the war and had another child. She survived alone. It wasn't a rare story in Israel in those days. Michael had been reduced by immigration, losing his status and employment prospects in this harsh new country. He became a house-painter on the kibbutz. Isaac's mother, who was beautiful and glamorous, left him for someone else when Isaac was small. Isaac was Michael's only son, and all he had left.

Isaac wasn't a professional photographer yet, though he'd become one later on. But he already had his camera, a Nikon F2, in his hand much of the time. He was holding it as his father rode by. This became the first image of Isaac's remarkable photographic account of the war:

After he snapped the picture, Isaac lowered the camera and called out.

Michael was overjoyed to see him. No one had known exactly where Isaac was, or if he was going to make it back. Other young men from the kibbutz had been arriving and disappearing into the war, and it seemed there were questions being asked about the ones who still hadn't shown up. Maybe not even asked aloud, but implied. These kids had been raised to fight. It was what the Jewish people required, so that what happened before couldn't happen again. Were they going to do what was expected?

Michael wasn't just happy to see his son again, he was relieved. He said something that Isaac never forgot, and which he repeated to me in a little kibbutz house a few hundred yards away from where this moment had happened forty-seven years before. He'd repeated the sentence, turning it over in his head, many times. His father said, "I'm so happy you came to the war."

Isaac loved his father until his death. He keeps a large photograph of him, one he took himself, on the wall. But he never forgot those words—the way his father was willing to sacrifice him, the idea that there were things more important than his only living son. It's an unsettling story, one of our oldest, from Genesis. If this were a novel, the character of the boy would have to be named Isaac, but in a novel you wouldn't dare call him that. It would be too much.

18

YUKON

Isaac was still en route when his friend Shlomi, the air marshal, made it to the front. He snuck onto a Tel Aviv flight against the orders of the officer in charge of security at Heathrow. Hundreds of Israelis were camped out on the airport carpets, trying to get home, there were threats of terrorism, and airline security personnel like Shlomi had been ordered to stay put and let the war take care of itself. Shlomi was enjoying London. Before he got the air marshal job he'd never been out of Israel, with the exception of the raids into Jordan, and had never flown on anything that wasn't an army helicopter. But now he'd been to New York and had seen Pink Floyd in concert. He could have exempted himself and stayed away. But he knew without being told that the men from Almond Reconnaissance, and Patzi himself, were going to reassemble, and he had to be there.

When he landed in Israel he took a bus to the big base at Julis, where reservists were signing up. He was still wearing the suit jacket he had to wear as an air marshal, an item of clothing that no one in their right mind wore in Israel, and he looked like an eccentric among the hundreds of men on the grass in jeans and sandals. Everyone was chatting and smoking, waiting for someone to tell them what to do. There was talk about the army forming a new tank battalion within a few days, no one knew exactly. Shlomi understood that this base was for people who weren't in a hurry to fight. Even though he'd already signed the papers making him a soldier, he jumped over a fence, which meant he was officially AWOL, and hitchhiked to his apartment near Tel Aviv. He kneeled by his bed to retrieve the rifle, uniform, boots, and helmet that he kept underneath, but there was nothing there. One of his roommates thought Shlomi wouldn't be coming back and had taken his gear.

The night was darker than usual because of the blackout. He started hitchhiking south, hoping to make it to Sinai somehow. He was standing by the side of the road near Ashkelon when he flagged down a bus that turned out to be carrying the famous entertainment troupe of the Fighting Pioneer Youth, heading south to play for the troops. They stopped briefly at a base where Shlomi looked for a tank battalion whose commander he knew, but the emergency warehouses were empty and the tanks gone. The only person there was a young clerk.

"Where's the battalion?" asked Shlomi.

"There's no battalion," she said. "They were among the first to reach the canal and there's nothing left."

Shlomi saw an Uzi lying around with one ammunition clip. He took it and continued southward into Sinai with the musicians. Their destination was the rear base at Baluza, which he knew as a place located a safe distance from the Egyptians, the kind of base you dream about when you're in the field—one with showers, chocolate bars, girls. But when they drove into the base, the speaker system was screaming for everyone to run to the fences and fire outward. The Egyptians were that close. It was the fourth day of the war. He'd assumed he was going to fight the Egyptians on the canal. If they'd penetrated this far, things were much worse than anyone was saying.

After a night manning positions along the fence, he caught a jeep to an encampment deeper in Sinai. Someone said Ariel Sharon was there, and Shlomi knew that if the beefy general was around, so was Patzi. If you wanted action and a commander who cared about his subordinates more than his superiors, you stayed close to Sharon. By this time, Shlomi had been travelling from London for two days straight. He walked among the prefab buildings at this new desert base and saw three soldiers kneeling by a fire, brewing coffee in a fruit can. Two were former Almond officers like Shlomi, and the third was Patzi himself, grinning under his blond curls as Shlomi approached. "I'll never forget that moment," Shlomi said. "It was as if someone had opened the gates of paradise and here were the angels and seventy virgins." Now he was in the catastrophe, where he belonged.

None of them had been given orders or even assigned to reserve units—they had just showed up—so they declared themselves to be their own unit. They already had one jeep, and Shlomi wandered off into the base and stole a second.

That's how "Force Patzi" was created, and became known to those who know, although officially no such unit ever existed.

On the morning of October 14, at about three a.m., a few Egyptian helicopters crossed the battle lines in Sinai and dropped a detachment of commandos near a point known on the Israeli maps by a Canadian name, Yukon. That was where the army had concentrated the big roller bridges that would be needed for the counterattack across the Suez Canal, if that became possible. It wasn't yet, because the Israelis were still reeling, and the Egyptians were about to send tank columns even further into Sinai. Israeli spotters saw the helicopters land and guessed that there were about one hundred Egyptian commandos in the desert near Yukon.

A few other Almond Reconnaissance officers had trickled in, finding their way to Patzi at this end of Sinai. One was Eitan, who'd rushed down from the engineering department at Ben-Gurion University, and another was Katz, who was unique for being an observant Jew and not an atheist kibbutznik. The improvised force picked up an armoured personnel carrier that had lost its unit, driven by a guy named Saul from Beersheba. Before dawn, Patzi's jeep led this crew out into the desert to find the commandos, Patzi on the machine gun, Shlomi at the wheel. Other officers might have found reasons to delay, call for reinforcements, or radio the air force and wait. The dozen men with Patzi would be outnumbered by a factor of ten.

They picked up a few tanks from a reserve brigade, the 600th, improving their odds. Shlomi remembers striking off the road into the desert following tracks, coming to a rise, then finding his jeep amid a mass of prostrate men dug into foxholes and concealed under the scrub.

It was as intimate as an ancient battle—you could touch the enemy and he could touch you. The Egyptians opened fire as Shlomi drove in. When the armoured personnel carrier driven by Saul from Beersheba came over the rise it was hit by a rocket that went right through Saul in the driver's compartment and then through Eitan, the engineering student, who was in the back. The vehicle just stood there discharging black smoke, but Shlomi only noticed that afterward, and barely registered the presence of the tanks. In his memory, he and Patzi are alone in their jeep. He swerves furiously, then reverses back down the dune and comes back up at another point along the rise, and Patzi starts shooting again. In and out, then back, firing at the figures next to the jeep. When the Egyptians shot at the Israelis in their midst, they hit each other. "We turned around and around and we killed and killed"—that's how Patzi described it to me when we spoke about this in his kitchen. "They died in their positions."

There's a 1,200-page regimental history of the 600th Brigade—a granular account of one unit's nightmare in Sinai compiled by one of the junior officers, later a university professor, Menachem Ben Shalom. The account includes testimonies from the tank crews who were there that morning, including the author himself. One of the tanks was quickly hit by a rocket, blinding the commander in the turret. The others charged into the mass of infantry. "We spotted the commandos," one crewman recalled, then changed to present tense, as if this were still happening, "and I attack with the machine gun and the treads, I'm crushing people and losing all semblance of humanity." A loader named Andrei remembered seeing "a man facing me with an RPG, and the order was given to run him over, and I remember the awful picture of the Egyptian soldier understanding that we were going to run him over, and I see the horror on his face as we run him over."

"One brave soldier of theirs suddenly stood up ten metres in front of the tank holding an RPG aimed right at us, right at my periscopes," remembered Ofer, a driver in a tank commanded by an officer named Yehuda Geller. The officer was exposed in the turret, speaking to Ofer over the intercom. "In those seconds I whispered to myself 'Hear, O Israel,'" he said, reciting the words of the prayer Jews say in the moments before death, "and waited for the worst. At that moment Yehuda Geller shot a few bursts at the soldier from the turret with his Uzi. My trance was broken by Yehuda's shout, 'Break left, crush him.' I turned left and ran over the brave soldier."

No one remembers exactly how long the battle lasted. The Egyptians fought almost until the last man. "No one surrendered," Patzi said. But the word *almost* is necessary because a few of the tank crewmen say there were enemy soldiers lying on the ground, maybe dead and maybe not, and Patzi shot them to make sure. There's a blurry time at the end of a battle when no one's certain it's over, and the blurriness can get you killed: maybe while one enemy soldier surrenders and you lower your guard, his friend shoots you in the back. That had almost happened in a smaller battle a few days before. Patzi had seen an Egyptian officer surrender then change his mind and raise his rifle. Patzi shot him first, and it confirmed what they believed in Almond Reconnaissance, which is that the battle is over only when you're sure that all the enemy soldiers are dead.

As the Israelis overcame the commandos, a few of the tank crewmen saw two or three enemy officers trying to surrender when Patzi killed them, too. This isn't how Patzi or his men remember it. Tank crews are trained to follow orders, to be part of the machine, and to do their killing at long range. They weren't used to close quarters and they hadn't seen someone like Patzi before. They thought he was berserk. The men who were in the battle describe Patzi with language that sounds less like Sinai than Troy. They were all soldiers, trying to do what they were forced to do, but he was born for it, something you don't see very often. He was the kind of person who wins wars for you and allows you not to know what that means.

When the shooting stopped and the desert fell silent, everyone could hear an eerie wailing over the scene, like a ram's horn. Only then did Shlomi look over and see the armoured personnel carrier smoking atop the rise. Saul from Beersheba was slumped over the horn. That was the terrible sound. Eitan's body was in the back and Katz, the religious officer, had lost most of his blood by the time a helicopter landed. Shlomi wrestled Saul's body out of the driver's seat, and the horn stopped.

19

AFRICA

There's a photo of Patzi from a few days later, taken by Isaac when he finally made it from Tokyo with his camera. The commander is leaning against the armoured personnel carrier. If you look closely, to the right of his head, near the top of the vehicle, you can see the little hole where the rocket hit. He's picked up a crude musical instrument left behind by Egyptian soldiers, a kind of improvised lyre, and there's a cigarette between his fingers. If you know the Bible you can't help but think of the beautiful killer with his secret chord.

One of Isaac's friends had given him a Russian rifle taken from the dead commandos. He had to clean blood off it. But his most important piece of gear was the Nikon, which he had out almost all the time. It wasn't just a way to record the events. The camera, he told me, was his shield. Years later, when his father was dying, he took pictures: "When I'm holding a camera it's not me." Few combat officers had cameras, and no press photographer was as close as he was to the fighting. It's thanks to Isaac's rolls of film that we can see what all of this looked like. Because he never bothered to register with the army when he landed from Japan, and just went to the front, he never officially served in the war, or with Force Patzi, which officially didn't exist anyway. Sometimes it's hard to believe that all of these things happened, or that he was there. But we have the photos.

In one shot Patzi is kneeling in the centre. Above him, with his hands on his hips, is Shlomi the air marshal. Isaac is the bearded one kneeling on the right.

Now the Israelis were finally recovering from the shock of the first week. The plan was to roll the dice with a canal crossing and a breakthrough onto the Egyptian side, which the

Israeli soldiers called "Africa." This would either end the war or end in disaster. The whole army was moving toward the canal, the roads through the desert jammed with trucks and commandeered civilian cars and buses. Isaac has a shot of that too:

In the foreground, with the cigarette, is an officer named Joshua, to whom Patzi gave the job of leading one of the first tanks to the waterline on the night of the crossing. The tank was hit by an Egyptian shell and Joshua was killed. Every so often the vehicles moving forward for the decisive battle had to pull off into the sand to make way for trucks bringing wounded back from the front. "A chaplain appeared on the roadside distributing copies of the Psalms," according to one historian, "which were snatched up even by avowed agnostics."

Isaac snapped a photo of Shlomi, the air marshal, cleaning a machine-gun barrel as they prepared for the push across the canal:

He has a photo of them plotting the route:

And taking a shower:

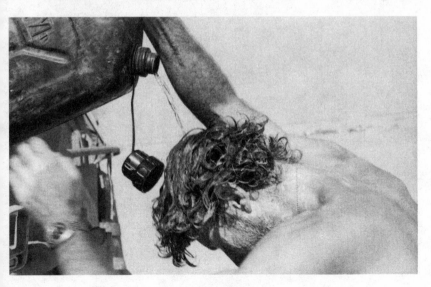

They tried to sleep:

But it wasn't easy.

The first troops crossed the canal and reached "Africa" without being detected. When the Egyptians figured out what the Israelis had done, the soldiers from Force Patzi found themselves at a cursed rectangle on the canal banks called the Yard. This was where General Sharon's forces were crossing, and it came under murderous shellfire. The general himself was lightly wounded in the head, and soldiers and engineers were being cut down in the Yard itself and on the fragile bridge over the canal. Isaac ferried casualties back a few miles to a clearing station—they'd load up their armoured personnel carrier with as many wounded men as could fit on the floor, race out, unload, then back to the waterline. Isaac remembers standing over five men on the floor, one of them screaming so loud that he had to ask him to stop.

In his memoir, *Warrior*, Sharon describes the Yard jammed with vehicles as shells fall. A tank pulls up, the turret opens, a young soldier climbs out. It's the son of Sharon's own signals officer, a middle-aged man sitting in the general's armoured personnel carrier. The father and son embrace, say a few words, and then the son goes off with his battalion into battle. An hour later word arrives that the son is wounded, and his father briefly leaves to find out what happened. His son's in critical condition with a spinal injury and can't move his legs, the signals officer tells Sharon, and goes back to work. The commander of the paratroops who were crossing the canal also had a son in a tank, and this son, too, was wounded. "All across the battlefield other fathers were losing sons and sons fathers," Sharon wrote. "Men who had fought in the War of Independence twenty-five years ago were still fighting." In his antiwar song "Story of Isaac," Cohen admonished the older generation for sacrificing the young. But here in Sinai things were more complicated.

Isaac doesn't have pictures of the bloody scene at the Yard. In his photos the Israelis are alive and grinning:

And the dead soldiers are all Egyptians:

That wasn't the reality, just the pictures.

Patzi led his little crew across the canal on the second day of the counterattack, and there was more killing as they pushed into Egyptian territory. It gets monotonous to describe it after a while. Isaac remembers flashes: an enemy tank swivelling its cannon toward them and his knees going weak because this was it, and then the Egyptian tank exploding, destroyed by an Israeli tank that Isaac hadn't seen. The unit storming a cluster of Egyptian tents, killing the soldiers inside—but he doesn't remember more than that, or doesn't want to talk about it. Of the whole war, he said, "I took photographs, I saw things I didn't believe I was seeing, I repress it all. My mother said that when I came back I sat for a week and didn't move."

What everyone remembers was that within days of the crossing they were near an Egyptian air base called Fa'id. It was late afternoon when a truck materialized like a hallucination, carrying one of the grande dames of Israeli song.

Yaffa Yarkoni was famous as a singer of ballads from the Independence War, forty-seven years old, and there she was, across the Suez Canal with the troops of the front line, before the army even really controlled the territory. Uniformed bodies were strewn in the sand not far away. She'd somehow managed to cross the canal with an accordion player, and she was going to raise morale or die trying. She was in jeans and an army shirt, an orange bandanna around her neck.

She stood on the rear ramp of Sharon's armoured personnel carrier and started singing as the general and his soldiers contemplated this emissary from an impossible world where there were women with orange bandannas around their necks. It would be hard to believe this actually happened if Isaac hadn't been there with his Nikon:

Sharon knew her from the '48 war, when they'd both been young, before he was a general and she a grande dame, before Israel was even a country. He went over to kiss her:

She was still singing, as the men tell it, when there was a roar overhead. A lone Sukhoi appeared in the sky and dove.

The general shoved the singer into the vehicle and lay on top of her. The Egyptian came in firing his cannon. Patzi stood there in the open, taking absurd shots at the plane with his pistol until Shlomi pulled him down. A few of the others were blasting away with their Russian rifles and one of them, Golod, was using the big machine gun mounted on the armoured personnel carrier. You could see the red circle of the jet engine as it pulled up and away, and Golod's tracers rising from the ground and flying right into the red circle. The plane faltered. The canopy shot off and there was a helpless human being suspended in the air by a parachute, floating down toward the people he'd just been trying to kill.

A few soldiers sped off and grabbed the pilot as soon as he landed. The enemy.

The Sukhoi crashed in the desert nearby:

The soldiers gave the pilot something to drink and handed him off to interrogators. Isaac and Shlomi and the others took his silk parachute to use as a tent.

Like many dates in this narrative, the precise timing of what happened next is blurry. Shlomi thinks it was the same night. He'd just returned to their improvised camp from a sweep through the desert to scrounge fuel cans for the jeep. He needed benzine but all he could find was diesel. The camp was a quiet group of dirty men, the jeep with its empty fuel tank, the armoured vehicle with the rocket hole and bloodstains, a few tanks. Some of the soldiers were eating combat rations near the parachute-tent.

They were somewhere west of Suez, a place Shlomi remembers as "nowhere": "Put your finger anywhere on the map. Dunes. A white parachute." Shlomi is not an excitable speaker. He's seen a lot, and he's efficient, not voluble. But here his story took on a different tone. As he approached the encampment, he heard a voice.

"It is," he said, "as if you're walking in the desert and God comes down to you and starts speaking. I was like Moses hearing the voice, and I walked toward it. I'll paint the picture for you: A steel helmet on the sand. Sitting on the helmet is a figure with a guitar, singing 'Lover Lover Lover.'"

20

BLOOD ON YOUR HANDS

Cohen and the band had flown across the canal into Egyptian territory that had just been captured, almost to the front line. The war was at its climax.

25. A helicopter dropped us on the African side of the Canal. This airport had been taken a day or two before. We sang in a concrete hangar. There was an Egyptian calendar on the wall and they had also left some food behind. I happened to be trying to get some sleep beside these tin cans. One of the cans, a giant-sized can of mashed potatoes said, A Gift from the People of Canada.

26. We had to take cover now and then.

27. Feeling good in the desert. War is ok. People at their best. As my friend Layton said about acid on his first 'trip': They'll never stamp this out.

In Shlomi's memory, on the night he saw him, Cohen was illuminated by the lights of a small truck. He had no audience and was strumming to himself. Maybe he was just waiting to be taken somewhere else. Or maybe he was trying to play but the soldiers were too exhausted or depressed to listen, or didn't notice he was there.

The Israeli knew who it was because he'd actually seen Cohen twice: first in concert in New York during one of his trips there with the airline, and then on an Athens–Tel Aviv flight before the war. When Cohen carried a guitar onto the plane, the flight attendant didn't recognize him and tried to make him stow it, and Shlomi intervened. They struck up a conversation, though the singer seemed guarded. "You feel that he's travelling in worlds that belong to him," Shlomi said. "His sentences were not constructed in the ordinary way. Sometimes he'd focus, but you didn't always feel that he was with you."

Here in the desert, Cohen gave no sign of recognition and didn't seem talkative. Shlomi was so surprised to see the singer in the war that he said nothing. He tried to call his friends, but they were hungry and tired and didn't know Leonard Cohen. So he just listened along with two or three other soldiers who drifted over.

Though Shlomi can't say exactly when this happened, or where, he knows what Cohen was singing: a version of "Lover Lover Lover" with a verse that identified with the Israeli soldiers. It touched him to hear those lines, to know that someone like Cohen had come all the way to Israel and travelled to Sinai and even crossed the Suez Canal to be with them.

The Arab states were arrayed against Israel, and most of the countries of Europe were now refusing even to allow supply flights to refuel on their way here. Israelis had a feeling of acute isolation. Cohen wasn't a plane full of weapons or reinforcements, but he meant something. The singer said a few sentences to his tiny audience. In Shlomi's memory it was, "You're all together, and you're here for one another, and it's so rare and touching to see it. It's amazing to be here with you and see how you're together without asking questions." Shlomi remembers those last words in particular, "without asking questions," which echo something Cohen once said about why he's drawn to armies. "I don't really have any desire to shoot anyone's face off," he told an interviewer. "But, given how lazily undisciplined, wild and greedy we all are, when you actually manage to get a few people organized into clean clothes, graceful marching patterns and a habit of discipline and obedience, I guess it's really some kind of miracle. And those are exactly the same kind of methods used in monasteries, or in any form of training. That notion of training has always interested me, and the army has traditionally been a place where young men are trained."

After that, Cohen left the encampment and drove off into the desert. A year or two later, after "Lover Lover Lover" was released, Shlomi heard it on the radio. "But the bastard changed the words," he said. The part identifying with the Israelis was gone.

Over the years, Shlomi tried to remember exactly what the words were. But it was nearly five decades before he heard them again, when I read him the verse I found in Cohen's notebook, the one where the poet calls the soldiers "my brothers" and says he's come to help them fight. When I was done, Shlomi was quiet for a few moments. He's always wanted to know why those lines were erased, he said. The change doesn't make him angry, just sad. He wants to love Leonard Cohen, and this interferes. He thought Cohen was really there with them, unlike the other artists who came to play, even the Israelis. Shlomi owns a bar in Tel Aviv and has spent his life dealing with performers. He thinks little of most of them. "A lot of people say they sang in the war," he said, "but actually it was just air force bases, and the next day they were back at Café Casit. Not Leonard Cohen. He was really there. He ate a combat ration with us. I opened a can for him. He was a human being."

That's why it hurt when Cohen pulled back. The man Leonard Cohen was on the Israeli side, and the song was written at an Israeli base, but the poet Leonard Cohen thought his words had to be bigger than the Israelis and bigger than the war. Later, when Cohen performed "Lover Lover Lover" onstage, he'd acknowledge where he wrote the song. But he'd tell the audience it was for soldiers "on both sides." At one concert in France he even claimed to have written it for "the Egyptians and the Israelis," in that order.

The nighttime encounter with Cohen is a strange memory. Isaac and Patzi, who were in the same encampment, have no recollection of it. The show everyone remembers happened shortly afterward, possibly the next day, at an intersection near the captured air base at Fa'id. Sharon had set up his divisional headquarters here as the army pushed into Africa and began to cut off the enemy forces who were now stranded on the Israeli side of the canal. No one remembers how Cohen arrived, just that he was suddenly there. Isaac got it on film.

In one of the photos, Cohen is singing with Rovina and Caspi:

And then just with Caspi:

Because this was Sharon's headquarters, and because the general attracted attention, there were a few cameras in the crowd. That's why, if you've ever seen a photo from a Cohen concert in Sinai, it's probably from this one. There was also a technician from Army Radio who can be seen recording the show; it's not clear what happened to the tapes. The photos help us imagine the many undocumented shows of the war tour—the guitar case on the sand with the name *Matti* in chalk, belonging to Matti Caspi; Cohen's military garb; the soldiers huddled around the singers.

Isaac photographed Cohen while crouching close to the singer. The best photo was taken by another soldier, Yakovi Doron, who was standing further away and caught the sweep of the scene. Doron was an artillery spotter who'd driven down from the hills, where he'd been radioing coordinates to the big guns dropping shells on the Egyptians below.

In this frame, General Sharon is to the left of Cohen, speaking to Rovina, who's standing behind the singer. The photo shows the concert, Doron told me, but not what was around them in the desert. Before seeing Cohen, he'd come across a unit of Egyptians who'd just been killed in battle, fifteen or twenty of them lying near a burned-out truck. He still remembers the smell. He snapped a few shots because he wanted to remember how awful everything was. They were on the same roll of Kodachrome slide film that he used to take photos of the concert, but he doesn't know where those photos are now.

The soldier next to Caspi, with the skullcap and his hand touching his mouth, is Eli Kraus, who was twenty-one. On the

day that Cohen appeared, he recalled, there was a pause in the action and someone came over with word that entertainers had somehow reached their camp. Many of the soldiers were too tired to get up, or didn't feel like hearing music. Eli was attached to Sharon's headquarters as part of a burial team commanded by an army rabbi. The team's job was to go to the battlefields and pick up the dead. He'd already been at the Chinese Farm, one of the worst battles of the war, and in the bombardment of the canal crossing. At one point he drove a jeep all night from the front across the Sinai desert back to his kibbutz in southern Israel to see his wife. They'd been married for five months. On his way, outside a different kibbutz not far from home, he stopped at an army graveyard to drop off a body he had in the back. When Eli heard about the singers, he walked over to see. He didn't know who Leonard

Cohen was, but was excited to recognize Matti Caspi. An army photographer caught Cohen, for once, in the audience:

Cohen described it like this:

29. We drive toward Ismailia. We stop at the most advanced position. Desert landscape, tanks the only architecture. I am introduced to a great general, 'The Lion of the Desert.' I pay homage to his vitality and silently demand, 'How dare you?' He does not repent.
30. Men form a circle around us and we sing for them.

Sharon's first name, Ariel, means "Lion of God." There's a slightly different version of this encounter in another draft of the manuscript:

I am introduced to a great general, "The Lion of the Desert." Under my breath I ask him, "How dare you?" He does not repent. We drink some cognac sitting on the sand in the shade of a tank. I want his job.

It's unclear if Sharon knew who Cohen was, or cared. The episode doesn't appear in his memoir, and his son Gilead can't remember his father ever mentioning it.

In the audience, taking in the songs along with Sharon and with everyone else, was Patzi, fresh from the battlefield, not running the war like a general but fighting it with his hands. In this moment he and Cohen are two human archetypes, or two sides of our nature—"man of peace and man of war," as Cohen put it in "Story of Isaac." The singer who called himself "Field Commander Cohen" and his band the Army, for whom war was a metaphor or an ironic pose; and the blond field commander, for whom war was fresh terror and the corpses of real people, both friends and foes, lying in the sand nearby. The poet, the connoisseur of beauty and morality; and the man who employs violence to create the bubble of safety where poets can be oblivious to those actions or even condemn the people who have to take them.

"Israel, and you who call yourself Israel," wrote Cohen a decade later in *Book of Mercy*, his take on the Book of Psalms, "the Church that calls itself Israel, and the revolt that calls itself Israel, and every nation chosen to be a nation—none of these lands is yours, all of you are thieves of holiness, all of you are at war with Mercy. Who will say it?" he asks in a kind of prophetic rage, and without the self-mocking that makes most of Cohen's critiques tolerable. Cohen would probably reject the idea of any political context for the poem at all, but it was published after Israel's Lebanon war of 1982, when the country's image became more Goliath than David, and when the Western left began to turn against it in earnest. "Therefore you rule over chaos, you hoist your flags with no authority, and the heart that is still alive hates you, and the remnant of Mercy is ashamed to look at you," he goes on, working himself up. Years before, as a young and rebellious poet in Montreal, he'd condemned the empty ritual of the Jewish synagogue and was now condemning the empty politics of the Jewish state. "You decompose behind your flimsy armour, your stench alarms you," says the prophet. The heavens are angry "because you do not wrestle with your angel. Because you dare to live without God. Because your cowardice has led you to believe that the victor does not limp."

Patzi has little patience for war nostalgia or military histories. Today, as you'd expect, the field commander isn't a man of teary recollections. It's possible, without special effort, to imagine him taking over an infantry company at eighty. Decades later, it couldn't possibly matter which tank company went where, he told me, or which general said what. He'd never heard of Leonard Cohen before that day in 1973 and doesn't listen to his music now. So I was surprised to hear him say that seeing Cohen meant a great deal to him, and that he's never forgotten it.

I had hesitated when explaining what I was writing about, afraid he'd dismiss the idea as frivolity. Instead, he said he thought it was the only kind of thing worth writing about a war.

"What touched me very deeply," said the old soldier of that late afternoon in Africa, as the war entered its final week, after many horrors and before many more, "was this Jew hunched over a guitar, sitting quietly and playing for us. I asked who he was, and someone said he was from Canada or God knows where, a Jew who came to raise the spirit of the fighters. It was Leonard Cohen. Since then, he has a corner of my heart."

21

RADAR STATION 528,
SHARM EL-SHEIKH

Cohen next surfaces at the Sharm el-Sheikh airfield, near the radar station that was destroyed by Egyptian missiles on the first night of the war, and then attacked by mistake by Israeli tanks. The girls from the station, the ones who appear at the beginning of this book, were now in huts down by the runway, trying not to think about their friends. The rumours that the radar station had been captured, and the women raped, were still circulating and had reached their families at home. That wasn't true, but it was true that seven soldiers had been killed. Not all of their families knew. So many Israelis were dying that the army's burial and notification apparatus was overwhelmed.

A popular singer with long blond hair, Miri Aloni, arrived at the airfield with a few other travelling musicians and played "Song for Peace," a Hebrew protest song that includes the lines "Don't look back / let those who are gone go." That infuriated Pnina, the senior girl from the radar station. How could you say, "Let them go"? She gave three friends slices of cheesecake in their guard post, walked away, and never saw them again. These performers didn't know what the soldiers had been through. She never forgave Miri Aloni.

Ruti, the popular soldier who ran the telephone switchboard, the one who was friends with the dark-haired poet Doron, kept taking calls from Doron's mother and sister. They became more frantic as the days passed. No one was telling them anything, and the switchboard number at the airfield was the only one they had. Where was he?

He wasn't there right now, she answered, as instructed. She'd let him know they called. She said it again and again until someone must have told them, because they stopped calling.

Ruti kept writing in her diary and sending notes to her parents on army-issue postcards. These postcards had cheerful cartoons unrelated to what was actually happening in the war—a cheeky Israeli soldier looming like Godzilla over the Syrian capital, Damascus, or churning the Arab armies in a meat grinder. Ruti describes her young self as "very militaristic." She believed in the Israel Defense Forces. She wrote optimistic notes reassuring her parents:

> I don't have much to write. We're working hard and barely sleeping , but the feeling of self-sacrifice is so great that we don't feel tired. In general, you have nothing to worry about. You have to trust the soldiers and the pilots and this whole wonderful army. Things will be okay, I promise!

The night before, in her diary, she'd written:

I miss the ones who were killed.

In another postcard she informed her parents:

I forgot to tell you that right next to my office is the huge tail of a MiG-17.

This was one of the enemy planes shot down in the dogfight on the first day of the war.

I have a camera that I brought from home, and we're planning to take pictures next to the MiG in a thousand poses, because there's no satisfaction greater than that, than seeing things like that. When I saw it, the first thing I did was spit on it. By the way, the body of the Egyptian pilot is lying here near the base and it's—

Here the military censor has blacked out a few words, which she thinks were "broken into pieces." The last line reads:

Today Leonard Cohen is playing.

Ruti's postcard is dated October 20, the fifteenth day of the war. The truth is that Ruti didn't care about Leonard Cohen. She was more excited about the Israeli stars who were coming through the base almost every day. But Orly, the radar operator who copied poetry on her Perspex table, was so thrilled by the news that she fought to get out of a shift so she could see him.

The hall at the base could hold about two hundred people and it was packed. Orly was entranced. This was the first time she'd seen someone as famous as Cohen, someone unattainable, all the way from America. "He had this charm," she said, "you couldn't resist it, I think women can't resist it at all. He had something about him, something dark and mysterious."

Her most vivid memory of Cohen isn't from the concert but from her bed in the girls' barracks. It was a simple iron cot of army issue, over which she'd tacked a few poems by Rachel and a drawing of a mother and child by Ruth Schloss, the Israeli communist painter, which she cut out of a book.

One of the officers at the base, Tammy, came to her that afternoon and asked where Cohen could rest before the show. "I was dying for him to sleep in my bed," Orly told me. "Not with me, but in my bed. I wasn't there." She offered her bed nonchalantly, so that the other girls wouldn't understand what it meant to her, so no one would steal Cohen and offer him their own bed. She and Tammy brought clean sheets.

She sees Leonard Cohen's head on her pillow, underneath the drawing of the mother and child. Orly was nineteen at the time, and a grandmother when she told this story. "I didn't want any of the other girls to know who I had in my bed," she said. "I had his songs in my ears."

22

BATHSHEBA

Next to the airfield at Sharm el-Sheikh was a navy anchorage for gunboats and a few landing craft, the biggest of which had once lived a different life, carrying ore down East African rivers, with a different name, *Zambia Challenge*. When the Israeli navy bought the ship and refurbished it to carry tanks and infantry, they gave it a new name, but nothing warlike—*Bathsheba*, the name of the woman David fell in love with when he saw her bathing on the roof in the story from the Book of Samuel, retold later on in Cohen's song "Hallelujah." Three years before the war, the *Bathsheba* became infamous when a truck of explosives blew up on board and killed twenty-four people. A month after that, the *Bathsheba* was almost sunk at the port of Eilat by Egyptian frogmen with a magnetic mine, but survived to serve as the centrepiece of a hazardous mission in the Yom Kippur War.

Sharm el-Sheikh wasn't a paradise now. The Egyptians had mined the narrows and there was combat in the Gulf of Suez.

Two Israeli gunboats had raided an Egyptian anchorage on the other side of the gulf, sinking a few enemy boats and returning with a few sailors wounded and one killed. One of the lieutenants at the anchorage, Motti, remembered seeing that soldier wrapped in a blanket on a pier. He was eighteen and his name was Herzl. The helicopter wouldn't take him because there was only room for the wounded. Herzl just lay there for a while. Motti had a sailor in his own gunboat whose brother had just been killed fighting with the infantry elsewhere in Sinai, and everyone knew but him. No one told the sailor while they were at sea, going up and down the Gulf of Suez. They pretended nothing had happened. Only when they docked a few days later did Motti pull him aside. The kid asked how long everyone had known, and Motti squirmed. He was only twenty-one and hadn't been trained for this. That was the life of a young naval officer at Sharm in those weeks.

Another young officer, Roni, commanded one of the smaller landing craft and was preoccupied with preparations for something big, code-named "Green Light." This was to be a surprise invasion across the Gulf of Suez: The *Bathsheba* and the smaller craft were to cross the waterway and land a brigade of paratroops and a battalion of armour on the Egyptian side. They were going to go in like Omaha Beach if necessary, then come up behind the Egyptian forces facing the Israelis along the Suez Canal. It was a creative and perilous idea. Most of the attacking force would be aboard the *Bathsheba*, a lumbering target that could be sunk with one shell. And if the Egyptians were waiting on the beaches, there was a chance no one would return.

Roni's friend Yoram, another lieutenant, was chosen to land with the infantry as a liaison officer. This was not an enviable job and not at all what Yoram was supposed to be doing. His wedding had been scheduled for Tuesday, October 9. But the surprise attack came on October 6 and Yoki, the bride, saw her fiancé disappear into the military with all the other young men. They'd been together for three years, beginning with a date at the Comet Cinema in Haifa. Yoki doesn't remember the movie, just his hand on her shoulder.

Yoki was called up herself and sent to a logistics base in central Israel. For the first week she heard nothing. It wasn't like today. Most of the soldiers had no way to contact home, and they could be dead for weeks before you knew. When Yoki's cousin was wounded on the canal and taken to a hospital the family was actually relieved to hear it, because at least it meant he was alive.

By the end of the second week of the war, Yoki had still heard nothing from Yoram. She couldn't bear the whiplash that came with thinking they'd be married and then knowing nothing about his fate. She decided to go find him.

She got her parents to drive her to the airfield at Sde Dov, in Tel Aviv. She begged her way onto an army transport flight and was told to sit in the back of a small truck on the tarmac. The truck drove up the ramp into the Hercules, the ramp closed, and she sat on the truck's bench in the weak cabin lights and in the roar of the engines for an hour.

Two unexpected occurrences followed aboard the *Bathsheba* within about a day of each other.

In one, the open deck that was supposed to carry tanks to the invasion beach became the venue for a Leonard Cohen concert. The crews don't remember who brought him, just that he was suddenly there with a guitar. It seems likely that he came from the nearby airfield, where he'd slept in Orly's bed. Someone took a picture of Cohen on the ship in the sunshine. He's standing next to Roni, one of the lieutenants:

That was the first event. The second began with Yoki's arrival at the anchorage, looking for her groom. He wasn't there. But someone told her he was alive, as far as anyone knew, out on a patrol in the Gulf of Suez.

Then someone at the base decided that Yoki and Yoram were going to get married right now. People who aren't in wars think they have all the time in the world, but at

Sharm el-Sheikh in those weeks it was clear you just couldn't wait. It was time for the wedding.

The cooks threw together a few sandwiches. Someone found a bottle of wine and someone else improvised a wedding canopy. By a stroke of luck or divine providence, the rabbi of the navy was also at the base just then and was pressed into service. The speaker system told all hands to assemble at the dock, aboard the landing craft *Bathsheba*. Everyone came.

At sea, Yoram had no idea that Yoki had somehow made it to the southern tip of Sinai or that he was about to get married, and found out only when he reached the naval anchorage. Someone rushed him to the quartermaster's storeroom and got him some clean fatigues. In the girls' quarters they tried to get Yoki to wear a nice civilian dress, but she stayed in her own fatigues, dark green pants and a

khaki shirt. All the ships in the anchorage sounded their horns, and instead of just climbing aboard the *Bathsheba* from the dock, she was ferried out on a motor launch.

Yoram and Yoki were reunited on the deck where the tanks were supposed to go, where the ammunition truck had exploded, the site of the Cohen concert that happened around the same date as the wedding, though it's not clear which came first. After all the preparations for Operation Green Light, the mission was called off, and Yoram never had to land with the troops like Omaha Beach. The concert and the marriage ended up being the two most significant events aboard the *Bathsheba* in that war.

After the ceremony, the rabbi told them they had to spend the night together—that was Jewish law, and there were no loopholes. But when they went back to Yoram's room another sailor was asleep in one of the bunks. He'd come off watch exhausted and couldn't understand why they were waking him up, so they just let him sleep. In the end, Yoram went back to sea and Yoki flew out the next morning. The next time they saw each other was three months later, but they've never been apart since then. They have three children and seven grandchildren.

23

LET IT BE

When people in Israel say the Yom Kippur War killed the accordion, they mean that the music and culture afterward was different from what came before. The war discredited the old political leadership and the communal "we" and the approved soundtrack of folk songs and military troupes. But it didn't happen right away. The two most enduring songs written in the war were still in the old style—one trying to put a comic spin on things, the other offering communal solace and hope for better days. Both approaches are necessary and currently undervalued. "Send Underpants and Undershirts" is an amusing number in which a soldier gives his girlfriend a list of items to mail him at the front, reassuring her that he and his friends are "fighting like lions" and that when he gets home they'll get married. For a light song so out of step with the dark events, "Send Underpants and Undershirts" has had an impressive shelf life and remains popular.

The second song, "Lu Yehi," became not just the anthem of the war but one of the most beloved songs in the country's history. It started out as a Hebrew version of "Let It Be," with original words set to Paul McCartney's tune. The songwriter was Naomi Shemer, famous for "Jerusalem of Gold," which in the Israeli mind is indivisible from the lightning victory of the Six-Day War and the Jewish return to the Western Wall and the Old City. "Jerusalem of Gold" has a status similar to the national anthem. Her song from 1973, on the other hand, was a different kind of song for a very different war.

Shemer seems to have understood the phrase "Let It Be" to mean "would that it were"—in Hebrew, *lu yehi*—making it a kind of prayer, rather than a suggestion to leave things alone and let them take their course. Her lyrics are grim but hold out reasons for hope: There's a white sail still silhouetted against the black storm cloud. Sabbath candles still tremble in the window at night. She played the song for her husband, who was just back from the reserves. "He said, 'I won't let you waste this song on a foreign melody—this is a Jewish war, so give it a Jewish tune,'" Shemer recounted later on. Scheduled to sing on TV one evening during the fighting, she worked on the melody in the taxi and performed it in the studio. By the time she reached the Sinai front herself, many of the soldiers already knew it and could sing along.

The song seems to have had a remarkable effect at the time, opening a crack in the tough persona of the founding generation. When Shemer came to sing at a kibbutz that had lost eight of its sons in the war, for example, the members sat in a circle around her piano in the dining hall. Until then, no one at the kibbutz, Giv'at Haim, had publicly expressed grief. Sentimentality and self-pity were anathema to these people, who'd come out of the disaster in Europe and willed a Jewish state into being against long odds. When Shemer played "Lu Yehi," one member started to cry. Others followed. These were the kibbutz's first open tears, the first time anything like it had happened. "This song," Shemer's son has said, "gave people the chance and the right to cry."

After the ceasefire at the end of October, the Israeli chief of staff, Lt. Gen. David Elazar, known to all as Dado, came to pick up a file in the room where his secretaries worked. They had the radio on, and he heard "Lu Yehi," apparently for the first time. Dado had kept his composure throughout the catastrophe of the preceding three weeks, as other commanders and government ministers lost theirs. The prime minister, Golda Meir, called him her "rock." During the war, Cohen sent a postcard to his sister with Dado's craggy features on one side. He was dressed in an immaculate uniform, big fingers clasped on his desk, giving you the feeling that the country's safety was good hands. Later Dado was blamed for the war's failures and forced out of the army in disgrace.

When Dado heard the song in the secretaries' room, according to his biographer, he stood transfixed and listened. Then, forgetting the file he'd come for, he hurried back to his own office. A secretary followed him and was shocked to see the general at his desk with his head in his hands, sobbing.

The music that came after the war was less concerned with comfort or morale. It tended to be about the individual and the soul. The most talented member of the new school, and perhaps the only Israeli artist who is Cohen's equal, was the poet and singer Meir Ariel. As it happened, Ariel was a soldier on the canal in 1973 and came within a mile or two of Cohen as the war flared out with a final tragedy at the city of Suez.

"I took my guitar with me to Africa," Ariel told an interviewer after the war, "but I wasn't completely sure the guys really liked my songs, or if they encouraged me because they had no other entertainment." He developed an intimate style that later became his trademark, along with strange, smiling monologues that usually, but not always, remained on this side of lucidity. As the war drew to a close, his company was barracked in buildings on the southern edge of Suez City, near the canal, part of the encirclement of Egypt's Third Army. The soldiers grilled meat and talked endlessly. They looked at centrefolds in magazines sent by the wife of the Israeli president to the forces at the front, which they called "frontal pictures." They mixed vodka with grapefruit syrup and called it "High Explosive Cocktail." Ariel was seen dragging his rifle on the ground, holding its strap like a dog's leash.

Every morning, the announcers on the Israeli radio news would report, "Our forces at Suez had a quiet night." Ariel took that line and made it the name of one of his best songs, a train-of-thought description of a night in the life of a soldier: He's reading *Islands in the Stream* by Ernest Hemingway. He summarizes the plot. He compliments the Hebrew translator. He's drinking apple tea and smoking. Mindless pop songs are on the radio. There's a warning that an enemy squad has infiltrated. The moon pours bright light on Suez City and the sea. A friend shows up at the post and says: "Your time's up." That's the whole song. There's no heroism or death, or even a battle. Nearly everything that happens in the song is in the mind of the soldier. It's one of the great modern war songs— the opposite of "Jerusalem of Gold." There's no army, no nation, no reason, no meaning, just a human in a war.

We can place Cohen near Suez City around this time thanks to Jacob El Hanani, who is now an accomplished artist in New York but was then a twenty-seven-year-old technician in the army reserves. Jacob hadn't showered in weeks and his hair stood up like straw. He was living in an abandoned fertilizer factory, an apocalyptic maze of concrete towers and rooms that had become barracks and makeshift toilets. Not long before, he'd been sleeping on a filthy mattress in SoHo, trying to draw, and before that he'd been in Paris, living on cheap sidewalk food, chasing an art scene that wasn't there anymore because everyone who mattered was in Manhattan. It was on Boulevard Saint-Michel and the Île Saint-Louis that he discovered Cohen's music. Cohen was still considered an acquired taste in America—it would be that way until the last years of his life—but in France they said in those days that if a girl had just one album, it was Cohen.

When the war broke out, he fought to get on a plane and eventually made it to Suez. He remembers spending hours on guard duty at night, hearing ominous sounds and see-ing strange figures flitting by. There were Egyptian soldiers around, deserters and stragglers trying to get back across the lines. One night they got an intelligence warning of an attack and they all took up positions at the windows of the fertilizer plant, swapping rumours about the Egyptians being so desperate they were going to use poison gas.

Nothing happened and instead, one night around the same time, a young driver from Jacob's unit showed up with a message. The soldier, Yehuda, was a pitiable character, barely out of high school. The army had picked him up and thrown him here, and he wanted to go home. Jacob heard him saying over and over, "I'm just a kid," repeating those words as if they were going to help. The kid didn't want to get up at night for guard duty, and once the older soldiers had to pick up his cot and dump him on the floor. The message Yehuda brought was that Cohen was here and everyone had to come.

Neither Jacob nor anyone else knew who he meant. The kid didn't know either, he'd just been given the message and didn't understand it himself. Half the people in Israel are called Cohen. Even if he'd said Leonard it wouldn't have meant much. There were about eighty men in the unit. Some of them spoke the harsh Hebrew of Israel's poor neighbourhoods, others knew Romanian, maybe Arabic. Jacob was from a middle-class family in Casablanca. When his comrades heard him speak French on the phone to his mother they laughed at him for putting on airs. No one, as far as he knew, spoke English.

They were ordered to gather in a damaged amphitheatre nearby, part of a defunct vacation village for tourists who used to winter at Suez. The soldiers were warned not to point flashlights upward in case there were enemy planes aloft, and to be careful on the paths around the fertilizer plant because the area was full of unexploded munitions. They were cursing:

Who wants to go hear Cohen, who is Cohen? The soldiers had already been forced to see a few army entertainment troupes, musicians who tried to raise morale and who sang "la-la-la in Hebrew," as Jacob recalled. They were tired of it. A few other units had been rounded up, and there were about 250 soldiers at the amphitheatre when Jacob arrived.

An army troupe played a few songs that didn't make an impression and then Leonard Cohen walked out on stage, alone, with a guitar. Jacob associated Cohen with the life of the cafés in Paris, with his own life in art, which was on a planet unimaginable from the banks of the Suez Canal. It was not possible that Cohen was here.

As he seems to have done in all the Sinai concerts, Cohen played "Suzanne," "So Long, Marianne," and "Bird on the Wire," which were his most familiar songs, at least to the people who knew his songs at all. There were few of those present at this show. The older reservists, the ones in their forties, had never heard of him. Some of the younger ones had, but even they didn't know much more than his name. We know that Meir Ariel, Israel's answer to Leonard Cohen, was somewhere close by with his company of paratroopers. There's no evidence that the Israeli was at the concert. But it's tempting to imagine the two of them in one place: Cohen onstage, Ariel listening and smoking in the back. What would they have made of each other—two poets of rare genius in the unlikeliest of places at the same time?

The concert was kept short because it was still dangerous to have that many soldiers massed outdoors so close to the front. When Cohen finished singing, he was escorted away and the units scattered. The men picked their way back down the treacherous paths, avoiding the explosives that were lying around, and went to sleep in the concrete rooms to wait for the war to end. While they were waiting, Yehuda, the kid who'd been sent to call them to see Cohen, who didn't know who Cohen was or what he himself was doing here, touched something on the ground that blew him to pieces. He was eighteen.

Around that time the ceasefire negotiations began, and then the ceasefire violations. Kissinger was running messages back and forth from Jerusalem to Cairo. Oshik heard Cohen saying, "As soon as the politicians are in the picture, I'm out." At Suez City the army decided at the last moment to push from the outskirts into the city itself, sending tanks and paratroopers down the main boulevard, underestimating the Egyptians as if the preceding three weeks hadn't happened. The convoys were ambushed and dozens of soldiers died before they could be extricated. Jacob could hear the battle from the fertilizer plant outside town.

The musicians in Cohen's improvised band left conflicting accounts of the attack. According to Oshik, they played at an airfield as the troops boarded Hercules transports to fly down to Suez. He stood singing next to the planes and thinks Pupik was with him, but not Cohen. "We got stuck at the airfield," he said, "and that evening the same soldiers came back. It would have been better not to see them." The musicians dropped their instruments and started running with stretchers from the helicopters to the field hospital.

Matti Caspi describes a nearly identical scene at an air base, but dates it to a week earlier and places Cohen there. "I remember a surrealistic image," he wrote. A Hercules landed and dozens of soldiers got out. Someone gave an order, they sat on the tarmac, and Cohen played "Bird on the Wire" with Caspi accompanying him. When the song ended they got on trucks headed for the Suez Canal. Another Hercules landed with new soldiers, and they played "Bird on the Wire" again. "Like a conveyor belt," Caspi recalled, "we stood there all day and Leonard sang the song to the soldiers landing, and then they'd get on the trucks." That evening the musicians took trucks over the canal, and found themselves carrying wounded soldiers on stretchers and loading them into helicopters. They realized it was the same soldiers they'd played for earlier in the day.

Whenever this happened, it seems to have been a moment when Cohen broke:

28.   Helicopter lands. In the great wind soldiers rush to unload it. It is filled with wounded men. I see their bandages and I stop myself from crying. These are young Jews dying. Then someone tells me that these are Egyptian wounded. My relief amazes me. I hate this. I hate my relief. This cannot be forgiven. This is blood on your hands.

24

WAR IS A DREAM

Before leaving the country, Cohen returned to Tel Aviv. It took him a few days to get his head in order and disentangle himself. In this time, according to his manuscript, he methodically violated the halfhearted vow of chastity he'd taken on the plane over—in Room 8 at the Gad Hotel with one woman, then on the beach, then again in Room 8 but with someone else.

33. I hang out in Tel Aviv cafes for a few days until I make myself sick.

34. I decide to leave Israel, but I must go to Jerusalem first. I will walk to Jerusalem. I get lost in the outskirts of Tel Aviv and find myself back on the street with all the cafes.

He gave up on walking to Jerusalem and instead took a bus. He was reunited one last time with Asher and Margolit, the couple he'd met on the plane to Israel, the ones who represented commitment to this place, and this tribe, and to each other. Margolit's pretty sister was also there. At dinner Asher said, continuing the theme of their dialogues, "You must decide whether you are a lecher or a priest." Cohen didn't want to be a priest.

The owner of a hummus joint in downtown Jerusalem, Meir Micha, remembers seeing Cohen in the street. Meir was also just back from the front and recognized Cohen because he'd seen him play in Sinai. Meir doesn't remember what he sang, just that he smoked Gitanes, blue, with no filter—"a cigarette with a message, the artist's cigarette." Jerusalem gets cold by early November. The limestone buildings glisten in the rain. He remembers Cohen walking alone, hands stuffed into the pockets of a long coat. Meir was too shy to approach him. But others did, as Cohen wrote: "People stop me and thank me here and tell me never to leave Jerusalem." But he left, of course.

The literary manuscript, which he typed after his return, ends with him back in the white house on the island with Suzanne and their child. "That is the end of the story," he wrote,

> except to tell you how she became beautiful, as if I knew. The wind keeps slamming my shutter and then throwing it open in order to expose to the night the pathetic sight of me at my table. Twice I've had to chase a thin dog away from the garbage. It is a fierce night. There is no question that the moon will survive the clouds. As surely as the brain can clear, she has become beautiful. As surely as the war is a

dream and the wounded men can't remember why, she has become beautiful.

The manuscript wasn't published, or even finished. After that Cohen rarely mentioned the war. The silence was not only a feature of interviews but also of private conversations, according to his close friend, the American writer Leon Wieseltier: "Leonard spoke about his most private experiences but never about his public ones," Wieseltier said. "He never talked about his participation in public or historical events." The reason, he thought, was that "it would have sounded vainglorious." That sounds right, though the answer might also lie in the belief that his poetry would be reduced by a connection to real events. It's also possible that Cohen's appearance on the Israeli side in the war contradicted his desire for independence from any side at all, and his suspicion of political programs—"Just according to whose plan?" And it's true that attitudes toward Israel were changing in the years after the war, in part because winning, which Israel had just done at great cost, makes you less sympathetic. The politics became more treacherous.

The only interviewer who seems to have published anything of significance on the topic was the British music writer Robin Pike, who met Cohen in London less than a year later, in September 1974.

> PIKE: You mentioned that you went back to Israel at the time of the last war and you sang. Can you say a bit more about that? How did you actually take part?

COHEN: I just attached myself to an air force entertainment group. We would just drop into little places,
like a rocket site, and they would shine their flashlights
at us and we would sing a few songs. Or they would give
us a Jeep and we would go down the road toward the
front and wherever we saw a few soldiers waiting for a
helicopter or something like that we would sing a few
songs. And maybe back at the airbase we would do a little
concert, maybe with amplifiers. It was very informal and
very intense. Wherever you saw soldiers you would just
stop and sing.

PIKE: It strikes me as being rather dangerous. You didn't
feel any personal anxiety about being killed?

COHEN: I did once or twice. But you get caught up in the
thing. And the desert is beautiful and you think your life
is meaningful for a moment or two. And war is wonderful.
They'll never stamp it out. It's one of the few times people
can act their best. It's so economical in terms of gesture
or motion. Every single gesture is precise, every effort is
at its maximum. Nobody goofs off. Everybody is respon-
sible for his brother. The sense of community and kinship
and brotherhood, devotion. There are opportunities to
feel things that you simply cannot feel in modern city life.
Very impressive.

PIKE: Obviously you found that stimulated you. Did you
find it stimulated your writing at all?

COHEN: In a little way. But not really. I wrote a song there.

PIKE: Wars have in the past been times when people have written great things after or during.

COHEN: I didn't suffer enough. I didn't lose anyone I knew.

A month later, speaking with the Spanish writer Jordi Sierra i Fabra after a concert in Barcelona, the subject came up again. Here he's less patient.

FABRA: Why did you end the concert with a military salute? Why do you do this after each concert you give?

COHEN: Because I don't consider myself a civilian. I consider myself a soldier, and that's the way soldiers salute.

FABRA: But . . . a soldier? On which side? In what sense?

COHEN: I will leave that to your imagination. I am a soldier. That's all. I don't want to speak of wars or sides.

FABRA: Nonetheless, "Lover Lover Lover" is dedicated to your "brothers" in the Arab-Israeli war, and besides, you were there, singing for them. This indicates you're taking a side, and in a way, fighting for it.

COHEN: Personal process is one thing. It's blood, it's the identification one feels with their roots and their origins. The militarism I practice as a person and a writer is another thing.

FABRA: But you worry about war, and for that reason
it would be logical that you would be concerned about
both sides.

COHEN: I don't want to talk about war.

After that there's barely a reference to the experience in interviews, or any consideration by Cohen of what it meant to him. Anyone hoping for a hint had to be paying enough attention to his work to notice the song "Night Comes On," which appeared a decade later on the album *Various Positions.* By that time Cohen seemed like yesterday's man, and his American label famously didn't even bother releasing the album, though it included not only the enduring "Dance Me to the End of Love" and "If It Be Your Will," which might be his best song, but also "Hallelujah," now one of the most popular songs on earth.

Each verse in "Night Comes On" notes a chapter in the poet's biography: the death of his mother a few years before, unhappy domesticity, the wondrous arrival of his own children. It's a song about Cohen's intimate life with the people closest to him. Amid all of this, after a conversation with his mother at her snowy grave—

> *We were fighting in Egypt when they signed this agreement*
> *That nobody else had to die*
> *There was this terrible sound, my father went down*
> *With a terrible wound in his side*

He said, try to go on, take my books, take my gun
Remember, my son, how they lied
And the night comes on, it's very calm
I'd like to pretend that my father was wrong
But you don't want to lie, not to the young.

Nathan Cohen fought in the Great War as a lieutenant, one of the first Jews to be commissioned an officer in the Canadian army. He died when his son was nine, and Leonard Cohen really did treasure his books and his gun, a .38 revolver. Nathan's death came many years after his war was over, and the cause was illness. But here Cohen links it to the war that "we" fought in Egypt, which he seems to consider worthy of inclusion in a short list of momentous events in the life of his family.

Decades later, when Cohen's biographer Sylvie Simmons was working on her 2012 book, *I'm Your Man,* she asked him about the war. Cohen was in his seventies and less guarded. Now he spelled out, for the first and possibly the only time, the importance of the events of October 1973. The quotes didn't make it into the published biography, and Simmons was kind enough to allow me to publish them here.

"You seemed to have been drawn to violence," she said to her subject.

At times you seemed to be looking for a war—your journey to Cuba, or trying to join the Israeli army in the Yom Kippur War.

COHEN: Yes, I did. Just because of the sense of cowardice that drives people to contradict their own deepest understanding of their own natures, they put themselves in dangerous situations.

SIMMONS: As a test?

COHEN: A kind of test, and hoping for some kind of contradiction about your own deepest conviction.

Simmons asked about the impact on his life afterward. He said:

> After I'd been in this little war, which had a big effect
> on me, when I came back to Hydra after the war, and
> the experience of seeing what happens to people in war,
> I thought I'd try to make a go of it, of this situation.
> There was a little child, there was a nice house in Hydra,
> there was Suzanne, we had a history. And there was
> so much death and horror in the world, you know?
> I'm going to tend the little garden. It may not be the
> garden I wanted and exactly the flowers I planted, but
> it's my little garden and I'm going to do my best.

That might be what Cohen meant when he wrote at the end of his manuscript that his wife is beautiful again. The year after the war, Cohen and Suzanne had a second child, a daughter, who they named Lorca, after the Spanish poet.

25

WHO BY FIRE

Four and a half months after the ceasefire, an entry in Cohen's notebook places him in a hotel in the city of Asmara, which was then in Ethiopia and is now in Eritrea. He was working on new songs. He would never say that it was his experience in Sinai, at those intimate concerts where music was a matter of life and death, that restored his faith in what he had to say, or if in Israel he'd really found the place he imagined in his manuscript, the one where he could "begin again." That kind of explanation wasn't Cohen's style. If he'd lost his creative thread at thirty-nine it wouldn't have come as a surprise—most singers don't even make it that far. What's unique is that he didn't burn out, that he managed to resurrect himself. Had he faded that year, we would be without "Hallelujah," "Anthem," "Everybody Knows," and many other masterpieces. Anyone touched by those songs would be different had they never been written.

All that can be said is that in 1973, before the war, he was speaking about retirement and saying he wanted to "shut up," and that after the war he released *New Skin for the Old Ceremony*. One of the pleasures of going through Cohen's little notebooks is seeing words emerging from his head en route to becoming known to millions, like this scribble from the months of the album's gestation:

Wed.
Chelsea Hotel broken
I never heard you say:
I need you
I don't need you
I need you
I don't need you
& all that jivin around

Unlike his description of that renowned encounter with Janis Joplin in New York, his inferior poem about Aleece in Room 8 was never put to music, and the Gad Hotel never achieved the fame of the one in Chelsea. The hotel in Tel Aviv has been gone for years and is forgotten.

One page in the notebook looks like the start of a journal. It reads, "Imperial Hotel, Asmara, Ethiopia, March 21, 1974." Cohen reports eating an "excellent lunch at the Albergo Italiano," after which he washed his white shirt and hung it to dry on the balcony. He sang for an hour. "First two verses of Chelsea Hotel will do; delete the third." He rented a bicycle and bought grey fabric for a suit that would be ready by the coming Sunday. By four p.m. his shirt was almost dry, and he soaked his grey cords and hung them in the evening air.

Then, with a confusing jump in geography, these lines appear:

Hydra
March 1974
And who—and who shall I say is calling?

Two pages later, the embryonic form of the song appears:

> *Who by fire   who by water*
> *who in the sunshine   who in the nighttime*
> *who by stern command   who by his own hand*
> *who in the midst of love   who by the angry mob*
> *and who shall I say is calling*

Elsewhere you find this fragment:

> *who by earthquake*
> *who by heartbreak*

Cohen was riffing on Unetaneh Tokef, the medieval prayer that is recited on the Day of Atonement and which appears at the beginning of this book, the one in which a human life is said to be "like a broken shard, like dry grass, a withered flower, like a passing shadow and a vanishing cloud, like a breeze that blows and dust that scatters, like a dream that flits away." There are similar passages in the Buddhist tradition, in which Cohen was immersed: Our existence, according to the Diamond Sutra, is like "a bubble floating in a stream, like a flash of lightning in a summer cloud, or a flickering lamp, an illusion, a phantom, or a dream." The Jewish prayer goes on to list the ways those lives might end in the coming year, depending on how fates are sealed on Yom Kippur—by fire, water, wild beast, sword. It's the prayer that was sung in synagogues across Israel not long before the siren on October 6, 1973, sent thousands of people to their deaths by fire or water, scattering them like dust or dreams. Some of those people have appeared in these pages.

The ancient prayer had two remarkable incarnations after the war. Cohen's version, "Who by Fire," was the first. His song is now more famous than the original. The second originated on a kibbutz in northern Israel over which the war still hovers, as one member said, "like a black cloud."

"A few days after the war ended, rumours started flying around the unit," Amichai Yarchi, a soldier from Kibbutz Beit Hashita, said in an interview on Israeli television. The first rumours said the kibbutz had lost ten members, then eleven. It didn't seem possible. But after the ceasefire, eleven small army trucks pulled through the kibbutz gates, headlights on even though it was daytime. Each bore one coffin. The men were the kibbutz's next generation—young workers and fathers, most of them reservists who'd been called from their regular lives a few weeks before. Many people in Israel, and especially on kibbutzim like this one, hadn't observed Yom Kippur before 1973, believing their generation had progressed past archaic religion. After the war, Yom Kippur on the kibbutz became a day of mourning. "I have two Yom Kippurs," Yarchi said. "One Yom Kippur is the day the war broke out, and the other Yom Kippur belongs to the rest of the people of Israel and is passed from generation to generation. The Yom Kippur of the war was the end of an era and the beginning of a new era, one that I think Beit Hashita and the state of Israel haven't recovered from yet."

If Israel's music scene went in Cohen's direction after the war, away from the collective and toward the individual soul, the spiritual life of the country also moved toward his inclinations, abandoning the militant secularism of the founders for an openness to the old wisdom. Meir Ariel, the singer-soldier who was near Suez at the same time as Cohen, was born on a secular kibbutz but eventually drew close to Judaism and, like Cohen, wrote songs that can only be described as prayers. Others left Western civilization altogether for the world of unyielding Orthodoxy, like Cohen's bandmate Pupik Arnon, the comic. Rabbi Mordechai Arnon died at seventy-eight, not long after I interviewed him in his tiny apartment in Jerusalem, leaving six children and twenty-one grandchildren.

The grief of Kibbutz Beit Hashita was still raw seventeen years after the war, in 1990, when one of Israel's most famous songwriters came to stay. Yair Rosenblum had written dozens of hits, including many for the army's entertainment troupes, in the old Israeli style, a genre whose time had now passed. As Yom Kippur approached that year and the annual black cloud began to gather over the spartan kibbutz homes in the valley, he "decided to give something personal, something of himself, to this special day," as one kibbutz member remembered afterward.

At first he thought he'd write new music for Kol Nidrei, "All of My Vows," the prayer that is famous for opening the service on the eve of Yom Kippur, but whose Aramaic text is legalistic and uninspiring. Then he came upon Unetaneh Tokef, "Let Us Relate the Power," the same prayer that had inspired Cohen. The words couldn't have been further from the kibbutz's approach to Yom Kippur, which members had marked since the war as a day of meditation and honouring the dead, ceremonies unconnected to a God whose nonexistence remained an article of faith. In the prayer, humans are negligible next to a deity who is a shepherd and a righteous, fearsome judge.

"Yair read it and knew this was what he was looking for," the songwriter's friend, Michal Shalev, wrote afterward. "He didn't shut his eyes all night, and waited for the morning, for the house to be empty of people and for a chance to play uninterrupted." When Shalev arrived around ten a.m., she found Rosenblum "writing and crying." He played her a composition that combined European cantorial melodies, Sephardic tunes, and the music of modern Israel. "It was one of those moments when you feel shaken and an excitement that leaves no room for words."

There was a member of the kibbutz who had a good singing voice, and he performed the new tune when the community gathered that Yom Kippur. Rosenblum had introduced an unapologetically religious text into an atheist stronghold and touched the rawest nerve of the community, the loss of eleven sons in the space of three weeks. The result appears to have been overpowering. People started to cry. The tune made its way from that kibbutz to others, and then to synagogues across Israel, where it's now probably the most popular melody for the prayer marking the height of the Yom Kippur service. Part of the composition's power is the way it joins the two pieces of Yom Kippur in Israel: Jewish tradition and the war of 1973.

It's increasingly common, however, to hear the same prayer chanted to a different melody—the one Cohen wrote for "Who by Fire." This happened in my own synagogue a few months ago, and no one thought it was strange. The prayer had travelled from a synagogue somewhere in the violent world of medieval Europe to the placid Gate of Heaven in Montreal, where it was heard by a child in the 1940s, then mixed with his experience of the cultural tumult of America in the 1960s, and of a catastrophe in Israel. Then it migrated back into the synagogue.

The two incarnations of the prayer after the war, Cohen's song and the melody from Kibbutz Beit Hashita, were reunited as I worked on this book when an Israeli singer, Aya Korem, released a new version. Her song combined the traditional Hebrew prayer, sung to the melody composed at the kibbutz, with the verses of "Who by Fire," translated into Hebrew. The song braids the medieval prayer about life and death, the melody from the grief-stricken kibbutz, and the song by Leonard Cohen. These threads are now part of the way people experience the Day of Atonement. But in

Korem's song, none of this is explicit. An appreciation of what's going on in the lyrics and melody depends on how much a listener knows about the fearsome days of October 1973, when Cohen was in Sinai.

26

A BLESSING

The prayer that inspired "Who by Fire" is one of the three moments in the Yom Kippur service that have become linked, at least in my own mind, to this story.

Another moment occurs in the afternoon, when the congregation reads the Book of Jonah and its account of the wayward prophet's journey—not just his physical voyage from the land of Israel to dissolute Nineveh, but his trajectory from believing you can run away from God and fate to knowing that you can't. The book begins with Jonah escaping to the Mediterranean and ends with him immobile in the desert. He's been brought against his will to the attitude of the other Biblical prophets who respond to the divine summons by simply saying, "Here I am"—*hineini*. That Hebrew word appears in the Bible for the first time in the story of Isaac, spoken by Abraham when he hears God's voice. Abraham is about to be told to commit the most terrible act he can imagine. Saying *hineini* is the opposite of running away.

At the end of his life, Cohen released a song called "You Want it Darker." It's addressed to God. The theme is the futility of our manoeuvres in a script that we never write.

> *If you are the dealer, I'm out of the game.*
> *If you are the healer, I'm crippled and lame.*
> *If thine is the glory then mine must be the shame.*
> *You want it darker*
> *We kill the flame.*

The song was produced by Cohen's son, Adam, who was a year old when his father left Hydra to go to Sinai. The words are in English, except for one: *hineini*. If you listen to the track you hear that word sung by someone else, a rare appearance in a Cohen song of a male voice that isn't his. When Cohen reached back at the end of his life, he didn't go to his Buddhist monastery, to India, Hydra, French Canada, or the Village. He went back to the synagogue of his childhood, the one built by the Cohens in Westmount. The voice belongs to Gideon Zelermyer, the cantor at the Gate of Heaven.

The song includes a fragment from the Jewish mourners' prayer, the Kaddish: "Magnified, sanctified, be thy holy name." Some listeners, knowing what happened a few months after the song's release in 2016, believe that Cohen was saying the Kaddish for himself, that he knew he didn't have much longer. But Robert Kory, the singer's friend and last manager, remembers Cohen calling him up in the summer of 2015 to hear the first cut of the song. Kory made the short trip from his office in Beverly Hills to the poet's home in Hancock Park. Cohen was ill at the time, Kory said, but expected to recover. He was even talking about a new tour. Cohen played "You Want It Darker" for him in the living room. The song was a prediction of a sombre future not just for Cohen but for everyone. America was taking a darker turn, but there weren't many who felt it in the summer of 2015. Kory remembers feeling a chill in his bones, and asking Cohen if he couldn't come up with a brighter vision for their children and grandchildren. "I don't write the songs," Cohen said.

He never made it back on the road, and died shortly after the song's release. He was buried at the Gate of Heaven's cemetery, next to his parents. The same cantor read the prayers. Long ago, in "Lover Lover Lover," he'd asked his father to change his name, but the gravestone has the one his father gave him: Leonard in English, Eliezer in Hebrew. He never changed it.

The third and final part of the Yom Kippur service that evokes this story happens around midday, or just before the time the siren sounded on October 6, 1973. Men who are descended from the priestly class, who have the designation "Cohen" and sometimes that name, get up to bless the congregation. They remove their shoes as the priests did in the Temple, cloak themselves in their prayer shawls, part their fingers in the middle, and say: "May God bless you and protect you. May God shine His face upon you and be gracious to you. May God lift up His face to you and grant you peace." In Hebrew the whole thing is just fifteen words.

When, during his time in Israel, Cohen was drawn back to something, it wasn't just the synagogue or the tribe, but his specific place in the tribe. That's what Asher the proselyte meant in his trippy monologues about Cohen deciding "if he's a lecher or a priest," and when he wrote in his letter to the poet: "We believe that if you will receive the cape of the prophet Elijah, the Spirit of God will be on you to make you a real Cohen." It's what Cohen himself meant, in his unpublished manuscript, when he refers at one point to his "ruined Cohanic benediction." The subject was on his mind. As a child, he once said, "When they told me I was a Cohen, I believed it. I didn't think it was auxiliary information." When he grew up, he came to see the role of the priests as nothing but rote recitation, symbolic of the way dead ritual had replaced creative fire. You don't need to know anything to memorize those fifteen words. But the idea that an ordinary person, the grocer or the dentist, a person of no moral pretence, can be transformed for a moment into the cracked vessel of a divine blessing—this is, in fact, a beautiful idea. It's a Leonard Cohen idea.

Cohen's last reunion with Israel was in 2009. He'd turned his back on the crowd, retreating to the monastery on Mt. Baldy, and then, upon discovering that his manager had stolen his savings, came out to tour for the first time in fifteen years. That's when he found that he'd ascended to the upper reaches of fame and admiration, that he could fill stadiums around the world. His depression had lifted. Age had loosened the grips of his urges. He seemed happy. This is the Cohen we remember now—a wry lover in a fedora, a gracious envoy from a nobler time.

Just like Cohen's 1972 tour, this one ended in Israel. The venue in Tel Aviv was a few miles from the café where, thirty-six years earlier, the musicians had picked him up and taken him to Sinai. The café was gone, along with the old bohemians; today the site houses a generic coffee franchise where you can watch tattooed youth flash by on electric scooters. In the intervening years, Israel had abandoned the kibbutz and the collective ideal and moved toward Cohen, toward the individual. But at the same time, the world in which Cohen made his name, the one that once embraced people like Bob Dylan and Paul Simon and other Jewish kids escaping their parents for a culture that didn't care where they came from—that American world was fraying and looking treacherous after all. Tribes were reasserting themselves, extending their protection and suffocation. So by the time he returned, Israel was more like Cohen, and the world was more like Israel.

Tel Aviv was no longer a poor cousin of New York or Paris. It had somehow found its own Mediterranean sophistication and no longer needed foreign celebrities to feel cool. But people here were still beside themselves to see Leonard Cohen again.

The fact that Israelis have always considered Cohen to be a kind of Israeli is not only because he's Jewish. There are plenty of Jewish artists, and almost none with that status. It is, at least in part, because of the memory that at one of this country's darkest moments, he came. He didn't have to, and few others did. The story of Cohen in Sinai is one that people here know, even if the details have never really been clear. When tickets went on sale in Tel Aviv it was just minutes before the phone lines crashed.

As happened onstage in Jerusalem long before, when he was paralyzed by some sense of judgmental family, Cohen still couldn't see this as just another country to play in. At first he thought things were so complicated that he should probably skip Israel altogether, and changed his mind only when young Israelis flooded his manager's inbox with more requests than the staff could ignore. The idea was to do a charity concert whose proceeds would go to bereaved Israeli and Palestinian parents who'd lost children to violence and were working for peace. To further appease the savage politics of the place, he also announced a second gig in the Palestinian city of Ramallah, but those intentions fell afoul of the same kind of sentiment that drove the war of 1973. On the Arab side there were calls to boycott his show; people seemed to find his attempt at even-handedness as convincing as his claim, all those years ago, that he wrote "Lover Lover Lover" for soldiers on both sides. The Ramallah show didn't happen, and neither did peace. But fifty thousand people turned out in Tel Aviv.

Among them were many of the characters in this book. Orly from the destroyed radar station, who'd given Cohen her bed when she was nineteen, was there. So was her friend Pnina, the one who heard the enemy tank commander speaking Hebrew after the terrible mistake on the hill. They now had children the same age they'd been when they encountered Cohen the first time. They waved fluorescent green light sticks with everyone else.

Roni, the navy lieutenant who had his picture taken with Cohen aboard the *Bathsheba*, was there with his daughter.

Shlomi, from Patzi's crew of desert fighters, bought tickets but then didn't go. Cohen had sat next to him on a helmet in the dark on the far side of the canal. He'd been close enough to touch, and hearing him in a stadium felt wrong. Gidi, the young doctor who translated "Suzanne" and saw Cohen at a field hospital, was living in Canada and went to the show in Hamilton. He cried through most of it.

Shoshi, the Super Mystère pilot who'd seen the first concert in his dirty jumpsuit, was there. Oshik, the singer, by now a grizzled member of Israel's music pantheon, tried to meet up with Cohen, sending a reminder through a distant connection that they'd "slept together on the ground in Sinai." But Cohen was seventy-five and needed all his energy for the stage. Even the president of Israel couldn't get a meeting.

Whether or not Cohen really belonged to this audience more than to one in Nashville or Barcelona, the Israeli audience felt he did. The concert went down as one of the best ever held here, and people speak of it in almost religious terms, especially the very end.

After the encore, close to midnight, the concert diverged from the script of all the other concerts on the tour. Roni, the former naval lieutenant, recalls that the stadium "trembled." It was a *moment*—the Children of Israel were assembled at Sinai, something was about to happen, and here it was. It felt that way, even though what he was doing is clear only if you know about the war and the way he thought about his place in it.

Sept 2009

The stadium was quiet. Cohen raised his hands and parted his fingers. He switched from English to Hebrew—not the new Hebrew of the Tel Aviv streets but the archaic language of the synagogue and the Diaspora, of the old men at the Gate of Heaven, the language of the priests, fifteen words. He blessed the people, and left the stage.

p 196

1st song
"Dance Me To the End of Love"

"May God bless you . . .

ACKNOWLEDGEMENTS

This project couldn't have happened without the kind cooperation of the Leonard Cohen Family Trust or without the generosity of Robert Kory, the poet's friend, last manager, and the executor of his estate, whose insights into Cohen's personality and art were invaluable to me as the book evolved.

I'm grateful to everyone who shared their memories with me in my years of research—soldiers, musicians, and friends of Cohen, all of whom are mentioned in the text and source notes. Special thanks to those, like Ofer Gavish and Shlomi Gruner, who generously put their personal networks at my disposal; to Ofer and to Menachem Ben Shalom for reading the manuscript; to Isaac Shokal, for the wonderful photos; and to Rabbi Mordechai (Pupik) Arnon, who didn't live to read the final product.

I'm grateful to my Canadian editor, Doug Pepper, for understanding this idea from the first moment and making it a reality, and to Jared Bland of McClelland & Stewart for bringing it into the world of the publisher of Cohen's own works, one hundred floors above mine. Thanks to my American editor, Cindy Spiegel, for believing so deeply in the book, and to the excellent team at Spiegel & Grau; and, as always, to my agent, Deborah Harris, for following me down yet another rabbit hole and helping me out the other end. Thanks to the talented researcher Dan Magen for coming up with some of the crucial contacts that made the story what it is. Thanks to Peter Norman for the eagle-eyed copy-edit, to Leslie Camhi for the introduction to Jacob El Hanani, and to those who read the manuscript as it evolved: Nicole Krauss, Mitch and Tali Ginsburg, George Eltman, Jessica Kasmer-Jacobs, Benjamin Balint, Jonah Mandel, David Bezmozgis, Rabbi David Wolpe, Danielle Berrin, Yossi Klein Halevi, Jill Offman, and Bash Doran.

I've benefited greatly from the work of other Cohen researchers, but special thanks is due to Jeff Burger, editor of *Leonard Cohen on Leonard Cohen*, an indispensable compilation of interviews that I was lucky to find one day in the Strand in New York, and which ended up shaping my understanding of who Cohen was and how he changed over the years.

Thanks to my parents and first readers, Imogene and Raphael Friedman; to my sister, Sarah; to my wife, Naama; and to Aviv, Michael, Tamar, and Asaf, who don't care about Leonard Cohen but will one day.

NOTES ON SOURCES

INTRODUCTION

The description of Cohen's concert for soldiers in Sinai is from the defunct Israeli music periodical *Lahiton*, November 2, 1973 (Hebrew). No date is given for the concert, but the unnamed reporter writes that it was on the fourteenth day of fighting, which would have been October 19.

"'I just feel like I want to shut up. Just shut up. . . .'" Leonard Cohen speaking to Roy Hollingworth of *Melody Maker*, February 24, 1973. In the invaluable resource *Leonard Cohen on Leonard Cohen: Interviews and Encounters*, edited by Jeff Burger (2014).

"'For me, poetry is the evidence of a life . . .'" This quote, in Cohen's voice, was featured at a memorial concert held in Montreal in 2017: https://www.youtube.com/watch?v=yMxWjSpuefo.

CHAPTER 1:

RADAR STATION 528, SHARM EL-SHEIKH

The memories of Ruti Porper (née Avraham) are from an interview in Ramat Hasharon on November 21, 2019, and from Ruti's diary entries, postcards, and photographs. Some of her writing from the war appeared first in *Yediot Ahronot* in an article by Eti Abramov, "Things are good here. I miss the ones who were killed," September 11, 2013 (Hebrew).

I interviewed Pnina Biran (Lisser) and Orly Barkan (Sheffer) together in Herzliya on January 9, 2020.

Biographical details about Doron Lieberman, killed in the attack at Radar Station 528 (Mt. Safra) on October 6, 1973, are from a memorial book published by his family after the war (Hebrew). Additional details are from my interviews with Ruti Porper, Pnina Biran, and Orly Barkan.

"'I'll line my basket with Kinneret memories...'" From the Hebrew poem "Shai" (Gift), by Rachel Bluwstein, published 1930.

"At 1:51 p.m. one of the radios crackled at Babylon..." From the military history *For Heaven's Sake: Squadron 201 in the Yom Kippur War*, by Aviram Barkai, Kinneret Zmora-Bitan Dvir, 2013 (Hebrew), page 153.

"'The most important weapon in the sector,'" and the pilots' memory of watching *Tora! Tora! Tora!* are from Barkai, *For Heaven's Sake*, page 99.

Additional details on the attack at the Radar Station 528 are from a Channel 1 program from 2010 (Hebrew, reported by Yariv Mozer) marking thirty-seven years since the war: https://www.youtube.com/watch?v=GKzgAos-MoI.

CHAPTER 2: THE GATE OF HEAVEN

"'A large part of my life was escaping. Whatever it was. . . .'" From the documentary *Marianne & Leonard: Words of Love*, directed by Nick Broomfield, 2019.

"'I'd never been in a sunny place . . .'" Cohen speaking to Paul Williams of *Crawdaddy!*, March 1975. From *Leonard Cohen on Leonard Cohen*.

"'We cannot face heaven. . . .'" Cohen speaking at a symposium of the Montreal Jewish community in 1964: https://www.youtube.com/watch?v=cFMm_x1qlPY.

"'I live here with a woman and a child. . . .'" From Cohen's song "There Is a War," 1974.

"'Once, long ago, my songs were not sold . . .'" Cohen speaking to Alastair Pirrie of *New Musical Express*, March 10, 1973. In *Leonard Cohen on Leonard Cohen*, page 42.

"'It's over. . .'" From Cohen's interview with Roy Hollingworth of *Melody Maker*, in *Leonard Cohen on Leonard Cohen*.

CHAPTER 3: EGYPT'S BULLET

The Cohen manuscript is kept in the McClelland & Stewart archive at McMaster University in Hamilton, Ontario. I'm grateful to librarian Chris Long for assistance in locating the document, filed under the name "Unidentified—possibly early draft of My Life in Art." I learned of the existence of the manuscript from the footnotes of Ira Nadel's 1996 biography *Various Positions: A Life of Leonard Cohen.* I corresponded with Ira in 2019 and am grateful for his assistance.

CHAPTER 4: ACCORDING TO WHOSE PLAN?

"In Florida . . . a Jewish eye doctor . . . Another American doctor was operating on soldiers four hours after landing from Pittsburgh . . . A surgeon from Cape Town, South Africa, pushed onto a flight . . ." From the 1974 book *October Earthquake: Yom Kippur 1973,* by Zeev Schiff, translated from the Hebrew by Louis Williams.

"'At that time, before we had any political stances about Israel one way or another . . .'" From a telephone interview with Aviva Layton in Los Angeles, March 18, 2020.

"Soldiers in close formation . . ." From Cohen's poem "Lines from My Grandfather's Journal," in *The Spice-Box of Earth,* 1961.

"'I don't have to have a song called "Give Peace a Chance." . . .'" Cohen speaking to Alastair Pirrie of *New Musical Express,* March 1973. In *Leonard Cohen on Leonard Cohen,* page 43.

"'A lot of people who think that I've changed my religion . . .'" Cohen speaking to Stina Lundberg Dabrowski of Swedish National Television, in *Leonard Cohen on Leonard Cohen*, page 414.

"'Only nationalism produces art. . . .'" Quoted in *A Broken Hallelujah*, by Liel Leibovitz, 2014, page 77.

"'The Canadians are like the Jews . . .'" Cohen speaking to Paul Williams of *Crawdaddy!*, March 1975. In *Leonard Cohen on Leonard Cohen*, page 85.

CHAPTER 5: A WOUND IN THE JEWISH WAR
Excerpted from the Cohen manuscript in the McClelland & Stewart archive.

CHAPTER 6: MYTH HOME
"There's no point in starting a war right now" and other quotes from the Israel concerts in 1972 are from the documentary film *Bird on a Wire*, directed by Tony Palmer, released (briefly) in 1974, shelved, forgotten, and re-released in 2010.

"'I see Marianne straight in front of me and I started crying. . .'" From "Leonard Cohen Makes It Darker," by David Remnick, *The New Yorker*, October 10, 2016.

CHAPTER 7: BEGINNING AGAIN
"'Suddenly his manager came up to me and said Leonard wants to meet me. . .'" The anecdote and quote from Rachel Teri are from

"Like a Bird on a Wire," by Rona Kuperboim of *Yediot Ahronot* (Hebrew, May 28, 2009). Rachel, who now lives in Los Angeles, did not respond to attempts to contact her for this book.

Ilana Rovina was eighty-six and ailing when contacted by telephone on September 2, 2020, and did not remember any details of the Yom Kippur war tour. She died the following month of Covid-19. The recollection here comes from Matti Caspi's website, which includes a section on the war tour.

Oshik Levi's recollections are from an interview with him in Tel Aviv on June 6, 2018.

Mordechai (Pupik) Arnon's recollections are from an interview at his home in Jerusalem, July 6, 2018, and from several subsequent telephone conversations. He died on January 3, 2020.

The anecdote about the song "The Last Battle" comes from the Israeli music expert Ofer Gavish, based on the research of the musicologist Nahumi Har-Zion.

CHAPTER 8: WHO BY WATER
Ofer Gavish, now a music historian and tour guide, was a Phantom navigator in the 69th Squadron 69 at Ramat David. Originally from Kibbutz Yiftach. Interviewed in Tel Aviv on December 16, 2019, and January 2, 2020.

"The SAMs were like 'flying telephone poles . . .'" From "The Truest Sport: Jousting With Sam and Charlie," by Tom Wolfe, describing the air war over Vietnam at the end of 1967 (*Esquire,* October 1, 1975).

The navigator with the skullcap is Capt. Ze'ev Yogev Finger, who died on October 9, 1973. He was twenty-five.

The pilot Henkin is Lt. Col. Ehud Henkin, who died on October 7, 1973. He was thirty-one. His navigator was Capt. Shaul Levi, twenty-five.

Zorik is Brig. Gen. Arlozor (Zorik) Lev. He died on October 9, 1973, age forty.

Momo is Shlomo Liran, originally Shlomo Zaltzman, a Skyhawk pilot in Squadron 110 in 1973, later a prominent Israeli CEO.

The lead pilot Vilan is Avraham Vilan, then the deputy commander of Squadron 110 at Ramat David.

". . . 'heating and cooling a piece of metal three times a day.'" Maj. Gen. (ret.) Giora Rom speaking to Israeli public television (Hebrew): https://www.youtube.com/watch?v=1rnGpDOtABo.

CHAPTER 9: A SHIELD AGAINST THE ENEMY
Shoshi is Moshe "Shoshi" Rothschild, a Mystère pilot in Squadron 105 at Hatzor. Originally from Kibbutz Gvar'am. Interviewed on January 8, 2020.

"Pupik plays a senior officer surprising an addled new recruit . . ." This sketch is included on the 2004 re-release of Pupik's album *Kol Echad* (Phonokol, Tel Aviv).

"It was then, on the first day of the war tour, that Cohen wrote a song. . . ." Both Oshik and Matti Caspi remember him writing "Lover Lover Lover" between the two concerts at Hatzor. Giving additional credence to this version of events is that it was published during the war itself, in an article in *Yediot Ahronot:* "Macias hurried from the Lod airport to Tel Hashomer," by Emmanuel Bar-Kedma, October 22, 1973 (Hebrew). "At his first concert at an air force base, the singer was struck by great emotion, because of everything he'd seen and heard, and in the break between two concerts, at midnight, poured his feelings into a new song that he wrote, put to music, and performed on the spot." The song was "Lover Lover Lover." The article also includes a Hebrew translation of the missing verse, the one that appears under the title "Air Base" in Chapter 10, and it's clear from the article that Cohen performed this verse as part of the song. The precise date of the Hatzor concert is unclear, but it appears to have been around the end of the war's first week or the beginning of the second.

The notebook Cohen had with him during the war (catalog number 37-16) is kept by his estate in Los Angeles.

"Invoking this shield is what a Cohen does." For this insight I'm grateful to my friend and early reader, Cohen afficionado Jonah Mandel.

"Researchers studying the music of GIs in Vietnam . . ." From *We Gotta Get Out of This Place: The Soundtrack of the Vietnam War*, by Craig Hansen Werner and Doug Bradley, 2015.

Amos is Amos Bar-Ilan, a Skyhawk pilot in Squadron 110 at Ramat David. Originally from Kibbutz Ginnosar. Interviewed on January 8, 2020.

The concert at Ramat David took place on the evening of October 26, according to the informal "squadron book" compiled by Squadron 110 (located for me by the intrepid Ofer Gavish). The squadron flew its last mission of the war at two p.m. that afternoon.

CHAPTER 10: BROTHERS

". . . it appeared in an article written during the war by an Israeli reporter . . ." Bar-Kedma in *Yediot Ahronot*, October 22, 1973.

". . . 'the hottest furnace of the spirit today' . . ." Cohen speaking to Paul Williams of *Crawdaddy!*, March 1975. In *Leonard Cohen on Leonard Cohen*, page 81.

Biographical information on the two army privates named Eliezer Cohen who died in the years before the 1973 war comes from the Israeli Defense Ministry's memorial website, www.izkor. gov.il (Hebrew).

Details of Johnny Cash's time in Vietnam are from *Cash: The Autobiography*, by Johnny Cash with Patrick Carr, 1997.

James Brown's first quote ("where lizards wore guns") is from "James Brown, the Sultan of Sweat and Soul," *Washington Post*, December 7, 2003. His second quote ("soul brothers") is from *Jet*, June 6, 1968. Both appear, along with other details of Brown's trip to Vietnam, in *The One: The Life and Music of James Brown*, by R.J. Smith, 2012.

CHAPTER 11: IN THE DESERT
"One navigator on a Hercules transport . . ." This is Uri Dromi, later a prominent journalist, interviewed on January 1, 2020.

CHAPTER 12: TEA AND ORANGES
"'I'm killing an arrogant Israeli officer . . .'" This quote from Cohen appears in Nadel's *Various Positions*. It does not appear in the manuscript I found, suggesting that Nadel used a different version.

Gidi Koren's recollections are from an interview in Tel Aviv on January 26, 2020.

CHAPTER 13: NO WORDS
Pupik's recollections are from my interviews with him in 2019.

"'There are those who sing laughing . . .'" Cohen speaking to Jordi Sierra i Fabra in October 1974. The interview appeared in a 1978 Spanish book titled *Leonard Cohen*. From *Leonard Cohen on Leonard Cohen*, page 79.

CHAPTER 14: ALREADY WET

The anecdotes from the singers Avner Gadasi and Yardena Arazi are from the article "40 years after Yom Kippur, artists return to the shows at the front," by Nadav Menuhin, *Walla*, September 13, 2013 (Hebrew).

"... had his leg nearly severed by shrapnel." This was Amotz Brontman of the Nahal Brigade Entertainment Troupe.

"'Where do you get to stand up and speak?'" From the article in *The New Yorker* cited in the notes to Chapter 6 from October 10, 2016.

"'A pessimist is somebody who is waiting for the rain ...'" Cohen speaking to Michel Field of France 2 TV, December 1992. In *Leonard Cohen on Leonard Cohen*, page 313.

"'You have a tradition which says that if things are bad we should not dwell on the sadness ...'" Leonard Cohen quoted in *Melody Maker*, June 29, 1974. From *The Ultimate Music Guide: Leonard Cohen*, published by Time, Inc. (U.K.), 2016.

"'When people think that a song has to make sense ...'" Joan Baez in the 2009 documentary film *Leonard Cohen: Live at the Isle of Wight 1970*, directed by Murray Lerner.

"'The kid said, "Okay, okay, big-time poet ..."'" From *I'm Your Man: The Life of Leonard Cohen*, by Sylvie Simmons, 2012.

"'In a sense, when someone consents to go into a mental hospital . . .'" Cohen speaking to Steve Turner of *New Musical Express*, June 29, 1974. In *Leonard Cohen on Leonard Cohen*, page 55.

"'I was afraid at first that my quiet and melancholy songs weren't the kind that would encourage soldiers at the front . . .'" From Bar-Kedma's article in *Yediot Ahronot*, October 22, 1973.

"'Another famous artist is the singer Leonard Cohen . . .'" From a Voice of Israel radio report during the war, preserved by the State Archive and uploaded to YouTube (https://www.youtube.com/watch?v=QxAVJg6mQng). The reporter is Yossi Soker. The segment of Cohen's quote beginning "Of course I have impressions" and ending with "collect material" appears in Hebrew voice-over; the translation back into English is mine.

CHAPTER 15: PSYCHOLOGY
From an interview with psychologist Joel Livne in Netanya, November 3, 2019.

CHAPTER 16: RESPITE
"'Dakota took us back to Lod. . . .'" From Cohen's manuscript in the McClelland & Stewart archive.

CHAPTER 17: THE STORY OF ISAAC
Isaac is the photographer Isaac Shokal, interviewed at Kibbutz Evron, February 21, 2020. Isaac's photographs appear here with his permission.

Almond Reconnaissance is my English translation of *Sayeret Shaked*, a unit of scouts attached to Southern Command. In the unit's Hebrew name the word *shaked*, "almond," is an acronym for *shomrei kav darom*, or "guardians of the southern line."

CHAPTER 18: YUKON
Shlomi is Shlomi Gruner, interviewed in Tel Aviv on February 11, 2020.

Patzi is Amatzia Chen, interviewed at Moshav Karmei Yosef, February 20, 2020.

Eitan, the officer who rushed to the war from Ben-Gurion University, is Lt. Eitan Nir, who died on October 14, 1973. He was twenty-three.

The wounded officer Katz is Yaakov Katz, known as Ketzeleh, later a leader of the settler movement and a member of Knesset.

Saul, who Patzi's soldiers picked up with his armoured personnel carrier, is Lt. Saul Afrik, who died on October 14, 1973. He was twenty.

The history of the 600th Brigade is *The Hours, A War Journal: The 600th Brigade During the Yom Kippur War*, by Menachem Ben Shalom (Hebrew, 2019). Ben Shalom was the brigade's reconnaissance officer. I'm grateful for his assistance.

"'We spotted the commandos . . .'" The soldier speaking is Nissim Shalom (from *The Hours*).

"A loader named Andrei . . ." This is tank crewman Andrei Friedman (from *The Hours*).

Ofer, who saw the Egyptian with the RPG, is tank driver Ofer Idan (from *The Hours*).

CHAPTER 19: AFRICA

The officer Joshua, who died during the crossing, is Capt. Yishayahu-Yehuda (Joshua) Katz, killed on October 15, 1973. He was twenty-four.

"'A chaplain appeared on the roadside distributing copies of the Psalms . . .'" From Abraham Rabinovich's *The Yom Kippur War: The Epic Encounter That Transformed the Middle East*, 2004, page 364.

The precise date of Yaffa Yarkoni's concert on the other side of the canal is not clear. But Patzi—who seemed to have an ironclad memory for dates and places—put it on October 18 or 19.

One mysterious detail about the Egyptian Sukhoi pilot in the photograph is that he's not wearing a flight suit. According to Isaac, some have suggested over the years that the prisoner was in fact an Egyptian artillery or air force spotter who was captured around the same time. But Isaac, as well as Shlomi Gruner, believe that this was the pilot, and he appears in the series of photographs that Isaac shot beginning with Yarkoni singing and ending with the destroyed aircraft.

"'All across the battlefield other fathers were losing sons . . .'"
From *Warrior: An Autobiography*, by Ariel Sharon with David Chanoff (1989).

"'I don't really have any desire to shoot anyone's face off . . .'"
Leonard Cohen speaking to Biba Kopf of *New Musical Express*, March 2, 1985. From *The Ultimate Music Guide: Leonard Cohen*.

CHAPTER 20: BLOOD ON YOUR HANDS
Cohen claimed to have written "Lover Lover Lover" for "the Egyptians and the Israelis," in that order, in a 1976 performance in France: https://www.youtube.com/watch?v=Aok5vpsWb4g.

Yakovi Doron's famous photograph appears here with his permission. I interviewed him at Kibbutz Yifat on February 20, 2020.

Eli Kraus's memories of the scene are from an interview with him on January 3, 2021. He lives on Kibbutz Sa'ad. I'm grateful to Shaul Ginsberg, Kraus's friend and my wife's uncle, for identifying Kraus in the photograph. The graveyard he mentioned was near Kibbutz Be'eri.

"'I am introduced to a great general, "The Lion of the Desert." . . .'"
This quote, which does not appear in the version of Cohen's manuscript that I have, appears in Ira Nadel's *Various Positions*.

CHAPTER 21:

RADAR STATION 528, SHARM EL-SHEIKH

From my interviews with Ruti Porper, Pnina Biran, and Orly Barkan, and from the postcards and diaries of Ruti Porper.

"'I don't have much to write. . . .'" Postcard from Ruti Porper to her parents, October 10, 1973.

"'. . . next to my office is the huge tail of a MiG-17.'" Postcard from Ruti Porper to her parents, October 20, 1973.

CHAPTER 22: BATHSHEBA

The naval officer Motti is Motti Kaganovich of Kibbutz Afikim, interviewed on February 14, 2020.

The navy crewman Herzl is Pvt. Herzl Elmalem, killed on October 7, 1973. He was eighteen.

The naval officer Roni is Roni Mor of Nahariya, interviewed on December 15, 2019. I'm grateful to Chuck Feingold for sending me the photo of Mor with Cohen aboard the *Bathsheba*, which led me to the stories of the navy personnel at Sharm el-Sheikh.

The naval officer Yoram is Yoram Dvir. His fiancée (now wife) is Yoki Dvir. I interviewed them together on March 19, 2020. Photographs of their wedding appear here with their permission.

CHAPTER 23: LET IT BE

The song known universally as "Send Underpants and Undershirts" is officially called "You Have No Reason to Worry," words by Thelma Eligon-Rose, melody by Kobi Oshrat, recorded 1974.

"...killed the accordion..." For this insight I'm grateful to the journalist and scholar Yossi Klein Halevi.

"'He said, "I won't let you waste this song on a foreign melody— this is a Jewish war, so give it a Jewish tune."'" Naomi Shemer quoting her husband, Mordechai Horowitz, in "The Story Behind 'Lu Yehi,'" Ynet, June 26, 2004 (Hebrew).

The event at Kibbutz Giv'at Haim is described by the historian Motti Zeira in his 2017 Hebrew biography of Shemer, *The Honey and the Sting*. The quote from Shemer's son, Ariel Horowitz ("This song gave people the chance..."), is from "The song that became a prayer," by Nadav Shragai, *Yisrael Hayom*, September 28, 2017 (Hebrew).

The anecdote about Dado hearing "Lu Yehi" is from his biographer, Hanoch Bartov, cited in Rabinovich, *The Yom Kippur War*.

"Cohen sent a postcard to his sister with Dado's craggy features..." In the archive of the Leonard Cohen estate, Los Angeles.

"'I took my guitar with me to Africa...'" Meir Ariel in an interview with Smadar Shir in 1979, cited in *A Biography of Meir Ariel*, by Nissim Calderon with Oded Zehavi, 2016 (Hebrew). I'm grateful to Nissim for his help in an email correspondence and conversation in August 2020.

"...'frontal pictures'... 'High Explosive Cocktail'..." From a Meir Ariel monologue before a performance of "Our Forces in Sinai Had a Quiet Night" (Hebrew, 1996): https://www.youtube.com/watch?v=Zx_TsjQG3Fk.

"Ariel was seen dragging his rifle on the ground..." From Calderon, *A Biography of Meir Ariel*.

Jacob El Hanani's recollections are from an interview at his studio in New York on November 12, 2019.

The soldier Yehuda is Pvt. Yehuda Komemi, who died on December 12, 1973. He was eighteen.

"'As soon as the politicians are in the picture, I'm out....'" From Rona Kuperboim's 2009 article in *Yediot Ahronot*.

"'I remember a surrealistic image....'" From Matti Caspi's official website (Hebrew).

CHAPTER 24: WAR IS A DREAM

Meir Micha is the owner of the legendary Jerusalem hummus joint Pinati. I interviewed him on November 27, 2019. I'm grateful to Gideon Zelermyer, cantor of Sha'ar Hashomayim in Montreal, for the tip that Meir saw Cohen in 1973.

"'Leonard spoke about his most private experiences but never about his public ones...'" I interviewed Leon Wieseltier on March 19 and 22, 2020.

Cohen's interview with Robin Pike of the U.K. music magazine *ZigZag* was published on September 15, 1974. Reprinted in *Leonard Cohen on Leonard Cohen*, page 62.

Cohen's interview with Jordi Sierra i Fabra in October 1974 was reprinted in *Leonard Cohen on Leonard Cohen*, page 79.

"'You seemed to have been drawn to violence....'" I'm grateful to Leonard Cohen's biographer Sylvie Simmons for sending me the transcript of the exchange between them and allowing me to publish it.

CHAPTER 25: WHO BY FIRE
The notebook in which the text of "Who by Fire" appears is preserved in the archive of the Leonard Cohen estate in Los Angeles (catalog number 7-45).

The account of how Unetaneh Tokef was written on Kibbutz Beit Hashita is based on an article I wrote for the *Times of Israel* on September 25, 2012 ("A Yom Kippur melody spun from grief, atonement, and memory").

"'... a black cloud.'" From my 2012 interview with Hanoch Albalak, the kibbutz member who first performed the song. Albalak died in July 2019.

"'A few days after the war ended, rumours started flying around the unit. . . .'" Amichai Yarchi speaking shortly after the war in footage used in Unetaneh Tokef, a 1991 Channel 1 documentary about Yom Kippur on Kibbutz Beit Hashita (Hebrew).

"' . . . something personal, something of himself . . .' Yair read it and knew this was what he was looking for. . . .'" Kibbutz member Michal Shalev, writing in a booklet published by the kibbutz in 1998, two years after the composer's death (Hebrew).

CHAPTER 26: A BLESSING

Details of Robert Kory's meeting with Cohen at the poet's home in Hancock Park, and of the machinations behind the scenes of the last Tel Aviv concert, are from conversations with Robert, Cohen's friend, manager, and executor of his estate. I'm grateful to Robert for the many hours he devoted to helping me get the story right.

"'When they told me I was a Cohen, I believed it. . . .'" Leonard Cohen speaking in 1994 to Arthur Kurzweil of the *Jewish Review of Books*, cited in Simmons, *I'm Your Man*.

PHOTOGRAPHY CREDITS

CHAPTER 1
Soldiers at the Sharm el-Sheikh air force base: courtesy of Ruti Porper.

CHAPTER 9
Photo of air crew watching Cohen at the Ramat David air base: from the air photography team at Ramat David, courtesy of Ofer Gavish.

CHAPTER 14
Photos of performers at the front: from the Israeli army magazine *Bamahaneh*, courtesy of the IDF archives, Tel Hashomer.

CHAPTER 17
Photo of Michael Shokal on his bike: courtesy of Isaac Shokal.

CHAPTER 19
All photos courtesy of Isaac Shokal.

CHAPTER 20

The first three photos of the concert appear courtesy of Isaac Shokal. The fourth appears courtesy of Yakovi Doron, and the fifth appears courtesy of the IDF archive (photographer: Ron Ilan).

CHAPTER 22

Photo of Cohen and Lt. Roni Mor: courtesy of Roni Mor (photographer: Yonah Sneh). Wedding photos: courtesy of Yoki and Yoram Dvir.

Matti Friedman is an award-winning journalist and author. Born in Toronto and based in Jerusalem, his work has appeared regularly in the *New York Times, The Atlantic, Tablet,* and elsewhere. Friedman's previous book, *Spies of No Country: Behind Enemy Lines at the Birth of the Israeli Secret Service,* won the Natan Prize and the Canadian Jewish Book Award for History. *Pumpkinflowers: An Israeli Soldier's Story* was chosen in 2016 as a *New York Times* Notable Book and one of Amazon's 10 Best Books of the Year. His first book, *The Aleppo Codex,* won the 2014 Sami Rohr Prize and the ALA's Sophie Brody Medal.